HOW
DREAMS
SPEAK

HOW
DREAMS
SPEAK

AN INTERACTIVE JOURNEY
INTO YOUR SUBCONSCIOUS

WRITTEN AND ILLUSTRATED BY
NICOLE CHILTON

WORKMAN · NEW YORK

Names: Chilton, Nicole, author. | Chilton, Nicole, illustrator.
Title: How dreams speak : an interactive journey into your subconscious /
written and illustrated by Nicole Chilton.
Description: New York : Workman, 2021. | Includes bibliographical references.
Identifiers: LCCN 2021003568 | ISBN 9781523511440 (paperback) |
ISBN 9781523511440 (ebook)
Subjects: LCSH: Dreams. | Dream interpretation.
Classification: LCC BF1091 .C56 2021 | DDC 154.6/3--dc23
LC record available at https://lccn.loc.gov/2021003568
ISBN 978-1-5235-1144-0

Cover design by Vaughn Andrews
Design by Orlando Adiao

Workman books are available at special discounts when purchased in bulk for
premiums and sales promotions as well as for fundraising or educational use.
Special editions or book excerpts can also be created to specification.
For details, contact the Special Sales Director at specialmarkets@workman.com.

Workman Publishing Co., Inc.
225 Varick Street
New York, NY 10014-4381
workman.com

WORKMAN is a registered trademark of Workman Publishing Co., Inc.

Printed in China
First printing June 2021

10 9 8 7 6 5 4 3 2 1

The future belongs to those who believe in the beauty of their dreams . . .
—Eleanor Roosevelt

This book is dedicated to those
who believe their dreams have meaning;
and to Dan, Jasper, and Maggie,
who give meaning to mine.

Contents

The Magic of Dreams

SHORTLY AFTER MY BELOVED DOBERMAN PASSED AWAY, I had a dream about a playful crow. It brought me a ball and wanted to play fetch. I obliged. The game went on for a bit, and then I woke up. As I often do, I wrote about the dream in my journal, then went about my day.

Not long after, I had an ah-ha moment that stopped me in my tracks: What if my dearly departed dog, no longer constrained by his weakened physical shell, had come to visit me in my dreams with newfound energy to play ball? Throughout the next few weeks, other animals continued to appear in my dreams, all with similar characteristics to those of my old dog: dark black fur (or scales), playful, protective, and slightly intimidating. They became companions during my slumbering state.

Whether these dream animals were truly my pet in various spiritual forms, I did not care. Through my dreams, I found comfort and happiness during a stage of immense sadness. I looked forward to going to bed at night, eager to see what form my Bogey would take next.

A few years later, my sister's dog Millie passed away. Millie was a shaggy mutt, and our dogs had been best buds. It had been a while since I recalled dreaming

of an animal visitor, but the night Millie died a pair of wolves appeared, standing on a hillside. I knew immediately that they were Bogey and Millie, and that Bogey was telling me he'd found her and she was doing fine. When I told my sister this, she started to cry. She wondered if she had received similar visits but couldn't remember them because dream recollection was a challenge for her.

Not everyone is able to recall their nightly adventures, but believe it or not, they do exist. Scientific evidence proves that everyone dreams—remembering them the next morning is the hard part. Being able to recall dreams vividly is a gift, and one you should give to yourself.

This book was born out of creative necessity. I have been writing my dreams down for decades, but it wasn't until a mentor encouraged me to incorporate art into my dream writing that I started truly seeing themes, color palettes, and blurred lines between waking and dreaming. Because of this endeavor, I've had endless wells of project ideas, I've become more empathetic, and I always have a good story to tell.

Dreams speak to us. They are messages from our subconscious minds, communicating both abstractly and metaphorically. They are keys that unlock the mysteries our waking brains simply cannot process during the day. The better you can recall your dreams, the easier you can connect with yourself and the world around you on a more intuitive and creative level.

Perhaps you are the type of person who grasps at those gossamer strands of your dreams every morning, desperately trying to recall what just happened. Or maybe you listen with envy as a friend talks about a vivid dream they had, yet you never seem to remember any of yours. You might be one of those lucky beings who has clear and lucid dreams, often confusing what occurred during sleep with waking life. Wherever you are on your dream journey, I am excited that this book is now in your hands.

Because each human is unique, this is not a one-size-fits-all dream dictionary. The interpretations of the dream symbols and themes within these pages are not unique to me—they've been developed over thousands of years.

Dreams have always held a significant purpose in peoples' identities and spirituality; the depth and power of dreams across the globe is rich and full of wisdom. While I can offer only a brief glimpse of the importance of dreams across cultures, it is vital that we value the various traditions and beliefs of Indigenous peoples and understand just how much of our contemporary knowledge of their existence comes from colonialism and, in turn, much suffering.

In addition to recognizing and highlighting the importance of dreams the world over, I've looked at the symbols through a historical and psychological lens and included a dash of my own intuition. I hope you'll find this to be a helpful tool in your own dreamwork. If this is all still too intimidating, worry not! I have provided tips and techniques to help you enhance your nightly dreams, as well as brief backgrounds on the history and science of sleep. There's also a reference list of additional reading in the back if you'd like to dive deeper into dream research.

The world needs dreamers like you, or like the dreamer you can become. More importantly, *you* need a dreamer like you.

Let's get started, and sweet dreams!

Nicole Chilton

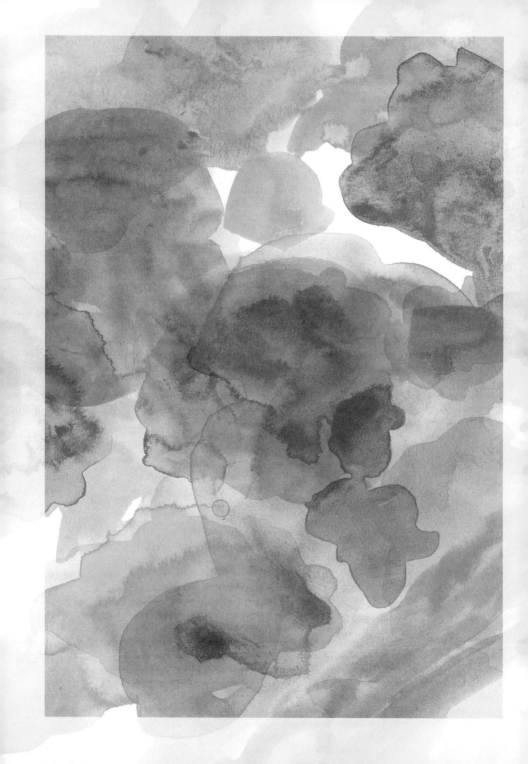

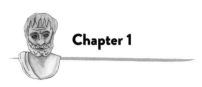

Chapter 1

The Philosophy of Dreams

WE ALL DREAM. Science has shown this to be the case, with the exception of those who suffer from certain neurological disorders. In 2015, French scientists studied more than two hundred people who claimed they didn't dream or at least couldn't remember dreaming. The scientists found that even though the subjects did not recall their dreams upon waking, each of them exhibited patterns and responses, such as muscle twitching and vocalization during rapid eye movement (REM) sleep, common to all dreamers. Even people who have been born with congenital blindness still experience REM sleep and recall dreams as tactile and audible experiences rather than visual ones.

Dreams are there whether you remember them or not. The more pressing question is *why* do we dream? And that's a harder one to answer.

Dreams aren't just wacky stories you tell your friend the next day. Historically, dreams could make or break a person—take biblical Joseph, whose brothers sold him into slavery after he boasted about ruling over them in a dream. It was a widespread belief in ancient cultures that dreams were direct messages from the gods. Ancient Greeks and Egyptians built temples for people to sleep in, hoping that a deity would visit them in their dreams. If a god or goddess made an

Ancient Greeks and Egyptians built temples for people to sleep in, hoping that a deity would visit them in their dreams.

appearance, they believed they would then be healed from an illness or instructed on how to solve problems in their waking life.

Many Indigenous cultures spanning the globe, in both the past and the present, use dreams for daily guidance and problem-solving, as well as to maintain a spiritual connection with their ancestors.

The Haudenosaunee (the people of the six nations in the Iroquois Confederacy and the original inhabitants of the Great Lakes region of North America) have long used dream incubation to help summon gods. Those who receive the messages are then initiated into the False Face Society, a sacred medicinal society. Members of the society are tasked with carving a mask from a living tree and performing healing ceremonies. The masks and ceremonies surrounding the False Face Society are so sacred that it is disrespectful to reproduce or sell the masks, as they are seen as living representations of spiritual forces. Dreams are also expressions of the soul's longings and a connection between the human and the orenda, a powerful spiritual force.

The Xavante, an Indigenous people in Brazil, consider dreams to be a sacred link between the natural world and their ancestors. Dreams are a way for elders to pass down their stories to new generations through ceremony and performances. Morning dream sessions are routine and help guide decision-making within the community. Even children's dreams are valid and listened to.

In the Western world, an early shift in dream philosophy came from the Greeks. Around the fourth century BCE, Greek physician Hippocrates started to link sleep and dreams with the physical body and explored dreams as a diagnostic approach to physical ailments. He believed when the body was at rest, the soul went to work performing all of the functions of the body. When vision is turned off, he wrote, the soul perceives the body's suffering and tells the mind through dreams. He would use these dreams to then prescribe a diet or regimen. For example, in *On Regimen IV*, he writes, "It is not good to see the earth scorched or black; there is a danger of catching a violent or even fatal disease, for it indicates excess of dryness in the flesh." His prescription: well-diluted white wine and plenty of baths. (We'll take it!)

Sigmund Freud

Philosopher Aristotle was another to separate dreams from the divine. *Wait a minute*, he thought. *Maybe our body has something to do with dreaming, not just the spiritual world.* In his work "On Dreams," he hypothesized that dreams were caused by indigestion or the continuing movement of our organs after we fell asleep. He was also an early thinker on what we now call lucid dreaming, or having awareness while we dream.

Centuries later, dream thinking shifted once again, this time from the spiritual and physical to the psychoanalytic. Sigmund Freud and Carl Jung led the way in the early 1900s. These two men were frenemies, both practicing dream psychology but with vastly different approaches. In a nutshell, here is what each thought about dreams:

Carl Jung

Freud believed dreams were repressed expressions of the subconscious. He used the example of the Greek myth of Oedipus to explain this. In the myth, Oedipus murders a man he didn't realize was his father and marries a woman he didn't realize was his mother (oops!). Freud thought this story showed how men have a primal instinct of deep love for their mothers and hatred for their fathers. Dreams, according to Freud, reflect repressed desires and allow a person to explore them through wish fulfillment. For any symbol in this book, or in any of the dreams you may have, there is a large chance that Freud would

Like the monarch butterfly that instinctively knows to migrate to Mexico, Jung believed humans have a well of shared knowledge, which he called the "collective unconscious."

say it ties back to sex, *especially* if it is a rigid object (phallic symbols), an animal with horns (denoting desire), or a vessel that can be filled (representing the womb). Bonus points if something explodes or drips (like a leaky faucet or a rocket launching)!

Freud's *The Interpretation of Dreams*, although groundbreaking at the time, has been hotly debated over the past century, in part because of its anecdotal and hard-to-prove nature but also because of its outdated approach that claims all women experience "penis envy." Feminist psychologist Karen Horney later critiqued Freud's theory and declared that perhaps all men experience "womb envy." Because these theories and interpretations closely tie a person's gender to their sexual organs, it's important that modern dreamers and thinkers develop a more inclusive and multidimensional approach.

Now, over to Jung. He was a onetime devoted follower of Freud and a psychoanalyst himself, but he looked at dreams a little differently. Rather than tying a dream and its analysis directly to sexual organs, he looked more at a human's psyche. Also using Greek mythology as a starting point, Jung realized that we have been telling similar stories (such as myths and fairy tales) that reflect our shared experiences since the dawn of human existence. Like the monarch butterfly that instinctively knows to migrate to Mexico, Jung believed humans have a well of shared knowledge, which he called the "collective unconscious."

When we dream, this shared knowledge appears as symbols and archetypes (models of behavior) we may not immediately recognize. Archetypes, according to Jung, show up as patterns based on four main categories: the Persona (traits put upon us by our social and cultural norms), the Shadow (our repressed desires and urges), the Anima/Animus (the duality of ourselves), and the Self (our unified whole). Within these categories, there are countless archetypes that can combine or merge with one another. Some include events (life, death, marriage) and figures (the child, the parent, the hero). Working with our dreams and these archetypes, according to Jung, can help us become better, more centered humans by acknowledging and embracing our anxieties, nightmares, and fears. We know we're on that journey when we start recognizing these symbols and archetypes from our subconscious and seeing them at play in our waking life.

Here, too, we must look at Jung's work through a modern lens: Archetypes study universal and instinctual patterns that he believed we all may experience. Because archetypes focus on such a big picture, our individual identities can sometimes feel at odds with them, so it's important that we look at these archetypes with a personal filter.

The study of symbols in dreams has continued to interest psychologists, scholars, and scientists, but with a more evidence-based approach. Dream studies have led to exciting discoveries on lucid dreaming, our brain waves during sleep, and emotional processing (more about that in the next chapter). But for a long period of time, dreams were either dismissed or heavily relegated to the study of parapsychology. During the New Age movement in the 1970s and 1980s, dreams once again aligned with spirituality. Followers embraced Western and Eastern spiritual beliefs and combined them with the metaphysical. The use of crystals, astrology, and dreamwork has helped (and continues to help) people seek a higher, enlightened state and feel connected to the universe. From ancient times to modern-day New Age beliefs, many people have believed their dreams are messages from the divine.

The use of crystals, astrology, and dreamwork has helped (and continues to help) people seek a higher, enlightened state and feel connected to the universe.

Think about your own personal connection to dreams and how they shape your emotional, physical, and spiritual life. Do you gravitate toward one of the various philosophies, or a mixture of them all? With dreams, there is no wrong answer or belief system. They are your experiences to understand and your stories to tell.

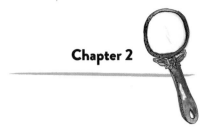

Chapter 2

The Science of Dreams

S INCE THE YEARS OF FREUD AND JUNG, neuroscience has played a more
prominent role in dream research. The main belief is that dreams stem
specifically from the brain and not from the spiritual realm or our collective
unconscious.

Before the 1950s, scientists thought that once we fell asleep, our brain pretty
much shut down. When brain imaging scans like MRIs (magnetic resonance
imaging) became more accessible, scientists began to finally, after centuries of
dreaming, see what was happening during sleep. Without even waking up a test
subject, scientists can tell from the sleeper's MRI whether their dreams are visual,
emotional, or motor-based. They've also learned which sections of the brain are
most active, which are not, and how that relates to our dreaming. Our rational
thinking hot spot in the frontal lobe, for example, is not very active during
dreaming, which explains some of the illogical events and timelines we experience
and take as truth in a dream.

Even with so many advances in scientific methods, thinking about why we
dream and what function it serves still remains a thought-provoking question.

Common theories include: that dreams are coping mechanisms from the stresses and traumas of our daily lives; that they are a biological response of a neurochemical process occurring only during sleep; that they are by-products of all the information from the day; or that they serve no actual purpose at all (well, that's no fun!).

Deirdre Barrett, PhD, a renowned dream scholar, blends a few theories together. During sleep our brains replenish biochemicals, but because our logic and reasoning aren't at the forefront, she posits that dreams can be a source of creative problem-solving. Barrett also highlights that dream interpretation is strongly based on the individual and that we should look at each dream through a personal lens.

Regardless of the theory to which you subscribe, scientists have found definitively that dreams happen during certain stages of sleep.

Stage 1: This is the transition between waking and sleeping, and it typically lasts about fifteen minutes. Your heartbeat and breathing start to slow, and your muscles relax. Your brain waves are in alpha mode, a calming and relaxing zone. A common dream sensation during this time is hypnagogia, where you might experience auditory hallucinations, like hearing people talking or music playing. I love to think that at this time, I'm tuning in to a cosmic radio, moving the dial up and down. If you practice meditation, alpha mode is a familiar spot for you.

Stage 2: Your body continues to relax, your temperature drops, and you enter a deeper sleep. During this stage, which lasts about twenty minutes, your brain experiences short bursts of neural oscillatory activity, or rapid brain wave activity. Known as "sleep spindles," these bursts have been correlated with learning and the accumulation of knowledge. Throughout a typical night, you spend the most time in stage 2.

Stages 3 and 4: Your brain waves, in the delta mode, slow *way* down, and this becomes the transition between light and deep sleep. If you want to feel like you've had a good night's sleep, this is the time period that makes or breaks it. This stage usually lasts for about thirty minutes.

Stage 5: Where the magic happens! Most dreaming occurs during REM sleep, although some can dream at other stages of sleep. During this cycle, your eyes start moving back and forth rapidly, and despite your being asleep, your brain activity, heartbeat, and respiration mirror that of your waking body. However, your muscle function decreases, leaving you temporarily paralyzed. This is a safety measure so you don't physically act out your dreams. REM sleep typically begins about ninety minutes after you enter stage 1.

In most eight-hour sleep sessions, adults can have anywhere from five to seven dreams during various REM stages, totaling about two hours.

> *What we do with our dreams and the stories they tell can affect our lives.*

In most eight-hour sleep sessions, adults can have anywhere from five to seven dreams during various REM stages, totaling about two hours. As you sleep, you will typically go through the stages in order, with each following REM stage lasting longer throughout the night and early morning. If you wake up remembering your dream, chances are you were in the middle of a REM cycle.

Whether you are attracted to the science of dreaming or love the idea that dreams are a cosmic connection provided by higher powers, the fact is, *we dream*. What we do with our dreams and the stories they tell can affect our lives. So let's put dreamwork into practice for the most important dreamer: you!

Chapter 3

The Curation of Dreams

RECORDING MY DREAMS has been a part of my daily routine since I was old enough to write. My first dream memory, from when I was about six, is a nightmare. A disembodied clown head would float around my room at varying speeds, then zoom at my face and laugh maniacally. Both horrified by and curious about the dream, I asked my mom to buy me a dream dictionary, which opened up a new world for me. Over the years, remembering my dreams has served me well.

Over the last few years, I've devoted a portion of my morning and creative time to really studying my dreams. The process has been eye-opening and has allowed me to start seeing the world in different ways. Throughout this project, I've felt more connected to the universe as a whole, unlocked a treasure trove of ideas, found new ways to solve problems in my waking life, and had a lot of fun exploring this fantastical world we spend a couple of hours a night visiting.

The best way to start learning more about your dreams is to write them down. Every day, if possible. The continued writing (and revisiting) will help you see themes, patterns, and symbols that show up over and over again. Here are some tips to help you get into the habit of dream recording:

BEFORE BED

THE DAY IS WINDING DOWN, and it's time to get ready for bed. Whatever your current bedtime routine includes, I have a few more items to add:

- Put your journal or recording device by your bed.
- Turn off your screens and electronic devices earlier than normal (at least thirty minutes before bed, if you can).
- Listen to some quiet music featuring binaural beats to help you doze off.

If you really want to amp up your dreaming, here are a few fun ways to enhance your nightly routine:

- Create a crystal pouch to put under your pillow.
  - Some great crystals to use in dreamwork include amethyst, fluorite, red jasper, clear quartz, and moonstone. These crystals are said to increase intuition and protect against negative energies (like nightmares!).
- Make a dream pillow.
  - Some herbs are known for their calming and relaxing properties. Create a little sachet of equal parts dried lavender and mugwort, which can assist with relaxing sleep and clear dream recall. Other dried herbs to experiment with include catnip, chamomile, jasmine, rose petals, and thyme. And if you want to "spice up" your dreams, consider a dash of cinnamon or cloves.
- Write down an intention to remember your dreams and place it under your mattress or pillow. It can be as simple as "I will remember my dreams." You can also repeat it out loud every night right before you fall asleep.

Sweet dreams!

i will remember my DReaMS

RISE AND SHINE

TRY NOT TO JUMP OUT OF BED as soon as your alarm goes off. Resist the urge to immediately grab your phone and scroll through your notifications. Distractions upon waking are the quickest way to lose the details of your dreams.

If you can, keep your eyes closed for a few extra moments. Remind yourself of what just happened in your dream world. If you wake up in the middle of the night, grab a pen and scribble away or record it in your phone. Some of my favorite dream journal entries are barely legible midnight musings. Picture the last thing you remember or an emotion you felt before being so rudely interrupted.

Is it there? Did your dreamscape come back like a thunderclap? Or did it blow away like a wisp of smoke? It's okay if it's gone. Lie still for a few more minutes before the bustle of your day begins. Even if all you remember is one feeling or image, record it. Later on, you might see a person or hear a sound that transports you back to your hidden world.

If the dream is still vivid in your mind, great! It's time to start your journaling process. To keep the thoughts flowing:

- Think in the present tense and first person.
- Go chronologically, if possible, although you may find that dreams don't always fit into a recognizable timeline.
- Sketch quick images or symbols that pop into your mind. Note that these may not fit into the overall narrative of the dream. Maybe the narrative isn't clear, and that's okay, too.
- Consider how you felt. Not how you feel in the present waking moment, but how you felt at each particular moment in your dream world. (If you are like me, as you are recording your dream the next morning, most of your thoughts are, *What? That's wild.*)

Consider how you felt during the dream. Not how you feel in the present waking moment, but how you felt at each particular moment in your dream world.

avocado

● ● ■ ●

"ahuacatl"
Aztec symbol for
love and fertility.
The fruit hangs in pairs,
"ahuacatl" translated to
testicles.

tough, leathery
skin, but
soft and sweet inside

avocados fit all the botanical criteria of a BERRY

• did you eat the fruit?
• did you pick it out or did   be fruitful
  someone give it to you?   (produce offspring,
• how did it make you feel?   or
• do you like avocados in   be productive)
  waking life?

for multiple insights I have been dreaming of
avocados (making avocado toast, stalking about
avocados, eating them #

● Every detail is important! Include colors, sounds, people, phrases, animals, and numbers.

You're a busy person, so penning a novel every morning about your dream is probably unrealistic. Get down what you can and let it marinate during your day.

Here's a peek at the questions I ask myself when I'm journaling:

1. Why did this symbol stand out among everything else in the dream?
2. How did I feel about it? Does this differ from how I feel about it in real life?
3. What or who could this symbol represent in waking life?

Remember, our subconscious mind doesn't think the way our conscious mind does. It is much more abstract and untamed, and it pulls from sources we may not know we have access to. The small details can be more important than we realize.

Finally, look at your dream and your responses through the lens of your waking life. Ask these questions:

1. How did this dream make me feel?
2. What is going on in my waking life right now that is on my mind?
3. Is there an obvious metaphor that I can see? (It can be as simple as a bug meaning something is *bugging* you!)

Use this book to help you explore some of the symbols that might have appeared. The more effort you put into recalling and recording your dreams every day, the easier it will become!

Chapter 4

The Variety of Dreams

BEFORE WE DIVE INTO THE SYMBOLS OF OUR SUBCONSCIOUS, let's take a peek at different types of dreams you may experience:

NUMINOUS DREAMS

THERE HAVE BEEN (OR WILL BE) TIMES when you wake up and feel that a dream has significance. Of course, all dreams are important, but these will *feel* different. You may have sensed a spiritual connection or had an ah-ha moment about something bothering you in waking life. It's like experiencing something so unexpected that it was clearly meant to be, for instance, running into an old friend halfway around the world. Jung refers to these dreams as "numinous," and after experiencing one, you may start transitioning into a new phase of growth.

Numinous dreams can also be prophetic in nature. While there is no current scientific proof that people can dream the future, you may be 100 percent convinced you saw a glimpse of something to come or a message from the beyond. It's okay to explore this! Write it down and work out the dream based on the symbols and your emotions. But remember: An action or situation that takes place in a dream is locked in symbolism. Dreaming about a death or tragic event doesn't mean it will occur—look at it as reflecting a metaphor or revealing a hidden emotion.

VISITATION DREAMS

DREAMING OF DEPARTED LOVED ONES can be powerful and world-shifting. Your loved ones might show up in different forms, such as animals or other people. It will be fairly obvious it's them, though, because of personality or physical traits. In these dreams, the departed tend to show up healthy and in their prime, and they are there to either deliver messages or say a proper goodbye.

Visitation dreams are similar to numinous dreams in that you awake knowing *something* special just happened. In a study about these dreams, participants said that having the visitations increased their belief in an afterlife and enhanced their connection with the departed.

SHARED DREAMS

WANT TO TRY A FUN EXPERIMENT? Ask your partner, best friend, or sibling to meet you somewhere familiar in your dream tonight. The first time I attempted it with my husband, we agreed to meet at a movie theater. While we didn't make it to our designated location, I dreamed of the staff from our favorite indie theater, and he dreamed of running the projector.

Shared dreams exist anecdotally only, and as of the writing of this book there hasn't been much scientific inquiry. But if we follow Jung's philosophy that humans share collective experiences, why can't we share dreams? Give it a try!

RECURRING DREAMS

RECURRING DREAMS, often in the form of a nightmare or an anxiety dream, happen repeatedly over the course of many nights, and often many years. One theory of why we have recurring dreams is that we have unresolved conflicts within our subconscious. For example, people who suffer from trauma or post-traumatic stress disorder (PTSD) tend to have recurring dreams and nightmares as a symptom. Revisiting these dreams and symbols can help us move forward with a problem.

Not all recurring dreams are scary or unsettling, though. As you go through this book and start a dream journaling process, you may realize there are many themes and symbols that pop up in your nightly adventures. I dream often about elevators but didn't realize it until I started writing this book!

AUDIBLE DREAMS

A 2016 STUDY showed that the majority of dreamers recall other people speaking to them the most, followed by hearing themselves. But what about hearing vivid music or noises that aren't part of your dream?

These hallucinogenic dreams tend to happen during the hypnagogic state of sleeping, when your brain is drifting into a calm meditative and transitioning state. Music, scientific lectures, foreign languages . . . it's a great place to be for inspiration. In fact, surrealist painter Salvador Dalí harnessed the power of this dream state to aid in his creative process, as did Thomas Edison and Ludwig van Beethoven. The scientist Dmitri Mendeleev even said he organized the periodic table based on a dream. That brilliant idea that came to you just as you dozed off? It might be the next big thing!

In the dream world there are no constraints, so you can do whatever you'd like. The sky is not the limit, and you can test out-there ideas, swim with sharks, or fly to the moon and back.

LUCID DREAMS

HAVE YOU EVER HAD A DREAM where you, as the sleeper, realize you are in a dream and can change or control what's happening? This is called a "lucid dream." Being a lucid dreamer is a great benefit for altering the course of your nightmares, and also a wonderful tool to help you develop better problem-solving skills.

In the dream world there are no constraints, so you can do whatever you'd like. The sky is not the limit, and you can test out-there ideas, swim with sharks, or fly to the moon and back. If you can't recall that you've ever had a lucid dream and would like to experience one, you're on the right track! One of the easiest ways to control your dreams is to start writing them down. Once you've gotten into that habit, add another mantra to your sleep routine: "I am in charge of my dreams."

The next step is to start testing your dreams. One easy way to do that is by performing "reality" checks during waking life. Look at the clock, read from a book, or count your fingers. If you can do it with complete success, chances are you're in waking life. If you look at your hands and suddenly they turn into lobster claws . . . well, you might be dreaming. Make this reality check another part of your waking life routine so that it might also become a habit in your dream life. Once you realize you are in a lucid dream, it's time to start having some fun! It takes a lot of practice to control your dreams, so don't give up.

ANXIETY DREAMS

THERE'S A THIN LINE between an anxiety dream and a nightmare. Throughout this book, you will find symbols common to anxiety dreams. (Raise your hand if you've had a panic-inducing dream about school!) Many psychologists believe anxiety dreams stem from childhood trauma, which may be the case for some. Chances are these dreams occur while your current waking life stress levels are high. During times of trauma, either individual or collective (like a pandemic or after a natural disaster), people tend to report more anxiety dreams related to the stressful event in their life. These dreams often morph into pure nightmares that revisit that trauma rather than speaking in metaphors, as dreams so often do. When processed healthily, anxiety dreams can help you reset your panic, work through what's causing you stress, and find logical solutions to help ease your burden.

One of the exciting parts of dreaming is that we experience events that can prepare us for real-life situations. If you become more lucid in your dreaming, you'll find ways to break out of these frustrating situations. It's not fun in the moment, but these dreams are begging you to look at and prepare for your days ahead.

NIGHTMARES

NIGHTMARES ARE COMMON IN CHILDHOOD and can have a long-lasting impact. (I'm still afraid of evil clowns!) These are the types of dreams that wake you up in the middle of the night, with your body covered in sweat, heart pounding, legs shaking. There can be many reasons why you experience nightmares: stress, trauma, illness, fear, even drugs and alcohol. As exhausting as nightmares are, psychologist Deirdre Barrett believes they serve a biological purpose, otherwise evolution would have knocked them out ages ago. She says nightmares create anxiety to prepare us for upcoming issues we may need to address. Lucid dreaming comes in handy when dealing with nightmares, as it gives you the opportunity to literally face your fears.

If the dream was particularly frightening and you woke up unable to move, you may have been experiencing sleep paralysis. Sleep paralysis is a common but temporary sleep disorder usually brought on by sleep schedule changes and extreme fatigue. Throughout history, people have described seeing an evil presence on their bed pinning them down, which spawned countless stories that keep people up at night. Just another reason to write down your dreams—it might inspire a hit horror story!

A final note about dreams and your health: If dreaming, or the stress of potential dreams, is causing sleep disturbances or insomnia, consider seeking professional help. Proper and deep sleep is vital for a healthy brain and mind.

In addition to these types of dreams, there are also a few overarching themes that may show up in your nightly travels:

PEOPLE

A PERSON IN YOUR DREAM doesn't always represent that person literally—they could be a symbol or metaphor. What traits did the people in your dream have? Are these traits some that you wish for yourself? Or perhaps ones you wish you didn't have?

People can also represent projects, ideas, emotions, or obstacles in your life. For example, a coworker who shows up in your dream may represent your job, especially if the dream doesn't take place in your traditional work setting. When this happens, be thinking about the traits that person has—they might clue you in to how you are feeling. If you want to think cosmically, you may be having a shared dream experience with that person. (Ask them to find out!)

It will be obvious to you if the person in the dream does genuinely represent that person in your waking life. Perhaps you've been experiencing intense emotions surrounding them, like anger, love, or longing; in this case, your subconscious mind may truly be working out unresolved situations and feelings. But do zoom out and think about those emotions. If you're dreaming constantly about one person and experiencing love,

maybe it's time to explore your own relationship with love as a concept, separate from that person.

With people in your dream, consider the following:

- How do you know this person in waking life?
- What personality or physical traits stood out?
- How did you feel about this person in the dream?
- What could they personify? A project? An idea? A relationship?

ANIMALS

IT'S SOMETHING SPECIAL when an animal shows up in a dream. They can be your beloved companions, visitors from beyond, or representations of a variety of major dream themes.

From a dream perspective, animals often represent our wild inner selves, the ones we don't get to unleash most days—and in dreams, the wilder the animal, the greater your need to unleash! Jung saw animals as a way to represent the conscious and unconscious worlds. He looked at their environments as a determining basis: soaring high in the clouds or living in the murky depths of the sea. The lighter and brighter the environment, the more it relates to your conscious life, and the darker and deeper it is, the more it is a symbol of your subconscious.

Spiritually, animals are viewed as guides and messengers known as psychopomps. A psychopomp is an animal or being that helps guide the recently departed to the afterlife. Just because one shows up doesn't mean you're on your way out, though! Notice what the animal is doing. Even if it's an animal you usually fear, a psychopomp is usually there to help you through a situation or protect you in some way.

After dreaming of an animal, pay extra attention if they cross your path in waking life. If they show up unexpectedly during your day (even in the form of art or references), you're most certainly on the path to learning something exciting!

Things to think about when an animal arrives in your dreams:

- What kind of animal was it?
- Could you communicate with it?
- How did you feel around it?
- What characteristics stood out, and which of that animal's traits do you admire?

NUMBERS

SOMETIMES A NUMBER IN YOUR DREAM will be prominent. It can be an actual representation of the number somewhere, or you may see multiples of an object or animal in your dream. Try to remember how many of that one thing you saw. It might be a clue as to what the symbol is representing in your waking life. For example, let's say you had a dream of three cats destroying your furniture. How many people do you live with? Did the number correlate? (Um . . . not speaking from experience!)

A shared language across cultures, numbers convey order, logic, and mystery. Certain powers have been placed in numbers, and through numerology it's believed that we can find balance and harmony between our world and the spiritual world. When numbers appear in dreams, break them down using the following formula and see if they have any significance. To do this, add all the numbers together until you get a single digit. For example, say you saw the number 417 prominently in your dream:

$$4 + 1 + 7 = 12$$
$$1 + 2 = 3$$

Numerology boils 417 down to the number 3, and studying the meaning of that number could give you a deeper insight into your dream's message.

Here are some qualities that are associated with numbers 0 through 9:

Zero: Nothing and eternality. Its round shape is full of potential, like a spiral or an egg. In tarot, it's associated with The Fool, a card of innocence and beginnings.

One: Oneness and importance. One represents the individual—unique yet unifying, with the capability of being built upon.

Two: Duality and balance. Two creates a whole through partnerships and relationships, yet two can also be divided.

Three: Spiritual and mystical. Three is full of creativity, connection, and completion. A number of life's groupings are in threes, including beginning, middle, end and past, present, future.

Four: Order and justice. Four is fundamental for stability and structure that comprises directional force (north, south, east, and west), the natural elements (earth, air, fire, and water), and our inherent human qualities (sensation, intuition, thinking, and feeling).

Five: Marriage and harmony. Five is representative of our senses (sight, hearing, taste, touch, and smell) and a physical representation of the points of the human body as well as the shape of the pentagram, a five-pointed star.

Six: Creation and perfection. Six is associated with the human body and the physical manifestation of love. With its representational balance of two triangles, it is a union of opposites.

Certain powers have been placed in numbers, and through numerology it's believed that we can find balance and harmony between our world and the spiritual world.

Seven: Celestial and contemplative. Seven is a highly recognizable number in our daily lives: seven days of the week, seven deadly sins, seven chakras, seven colors of the rainbow, and seven-day lunar phases, just to list a few. In tarot, it is associated with The Chariot and reminds us to pause before moving forward.

Eight: Infinity and balance. Eight is a number of the ongoing cycle of creation, birth, life, death, and renewal. The Arabic glyph *8* is similar to the symbol for infinity.

Nine: Completion and achievement. Nine is the final number before the next cycle starts, and it represents perfection, truth, and luck.

What to consider when a number seems especially prominent in a dream:

- What number is it?
- How did it appear?
- Have you seen this number recently or regularly in waking life?
- Does the number have a special significance to you?

COLORS

DO YOU DREAM IN COLOR? Colors have a deep symbolic history. Giving someone a rose of a certain color has its own secret language (page 121), wearing certain colors can make a powerful political statement, and some colors, like red and green, convey immediate universal messages such as *stop* and *go*.

When a vivid color shows up in your dream, consider the following, and then look to other details for further insight.

- How did the color appear?
- What emotions did you feel during the dream, and what emotions have you noticed yourself feeling lately in your waking life?
- Do you have any mental associations with this color?

Let's examine a few:

BLACK

TECHNICALLY, BLACK IS CONSIDERED THE ABSORPTION OF LIGHT, not a color. Because of this, it represents a void, the unknown, and mystery. In Western cultures, it's the color of death, in representational form and in mourning. The color has been associated through clothing with witches, artists, and anarchists, but also with judges and high fashion. When paired with white, it becomes a symbol of balance and dual forces, like with the yin and yang symbol.

BLUE

BLUE IS A VAST, SYMBOLIC COLOR, especially when tied to emotions. Think of the expanse of the sky and the depth of the sea. Blue is tied with political parties, classism (the aristocratic "blue bloods," for example), music, and emotions.

Even though it's a primary color, blue actually doesn't appear much in nature as a pigment. Because of its rarity and high cost in Renaissance times, the color blue was used sparingly in art to depict wealth and holiness. Later, when synthetic pigments were easier to come by, artists like Pablo Picasso used blue to convey—you guessed it—melancholy and despair.

GREEN

A COMBINATION OF YELLOW AND BLUE, green symbolizes abundance and growth and has become nature's unofficial color. In chakra healing, green is the color of the fourth chakra, located at the heart and dealing with compassion. Because of its connection to abundance and wealth, green can also represent greed and toxicity.

ORANGE

A BLEND OF PASSIONATE RED AND JOYFUL YELLOW, orange is often associated with creativity, sexuality, and balance. It's the color of the sacral chakra (located just below the belly) and of a burning flame. Buddhist monks use the color saffron in their robes as a way to remind themselves of their inner flame and true selves. Wearing orange has become synonymous with the movement to raise awareness of gun violence in the United States.

PINK

ASSOCIATED WITH ROMANCE AND LOVE, pink is the softer side of red. It has become an almost universally accepted symbol of baby girls and femininity due to modern consumers and marketing prowess. In the chakras it's sometimes aligned with the heart, and using rose-colored crystals helps one harness self-love and heal the heart. Pairing pink with white is a visual cue of youth, while pink combined with black is linked with eroticism. In Japan, pink is the color of springtime, when all the cherry trees blossom.

PURPLE

PURPLE, LIKE BLUE, is not a common natural pigment and therefore was historically extremely costly to use in art and clothing. Because of its value during the Elizabethan era, purple could only be worn by royalty. It wasn't until the 1800s that a synthetic purple dye was discovered and the color became more accessible.

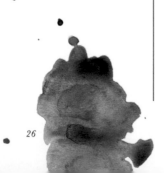

Deep purple and violet are the colors of the third eye chakra, an energy center located on the forehead. Your third eye connects you with intuition, wisdom, and dreamlike visions.

See also Amethyst (page 62).

RED
THE COLOR OF FIRE AND BLOOD, red is the easiest hue on the spectrum for our eyes to see. It's an emotional color, as seeing red can elicit immediate responses of warning, action, and passion. Wearing red can be a deeply symbolic choice: Because of its difficulty to reproduce in fabric, for ages it was used by people in power, such as cardinals in the Catholic Church. Red is also associated with fertility, so it is worn by Hindu brides. It is also a common theme in folklore (think "Little Red Riding Hood").

YELLOW
A BRIGHT, SUNNY PRIMARY COLOR, yellow's symbolism spans the spectrum. Its relation to the sun aligns it with royalty, and it was favored by emperors in Imperial China. It indicates courage and energy. In floriography, the language of flowers, a yellow rose can be a sign of friendship and caring. Yellow has another side, though, and is a cautionary color, warning people to slow down or stay away, as caution tape does.

WHITE
WHERE BLACK IS THE ABSORPTION OF ALL LIGHT, white is a reflection of all combined colors on the light spectrum. It is almost universally a symbol of peace, cleanliness, rebirth, and purity. Brides in Western cultures wear white, but in Eastern cultures the color is a symbol of mourning. Because of its association with light, white also indicates divinity—holy beings are often crowned with bright white halos.

PUNS AND WORDPLAY

Because the logical part of the brain is put on pause while dreaming, our dreams use metaphors and abstraction to bring ideas to the forefront. One way it does this is through wordplay, like homonyms and puns.

I once dreamed of driving a car filled with snow, and my feet couldn't warm up. In waking life, I was about to start a new job. The first thing I thought of was the phrase "cold feet," because my subconscious was pulling up hidden emotions of how nervous and unsure I was for this next *step* in life. Another example that I mentioned earlier is that you might dream of a bug if something is *bugging* you.

It's important, when you start writing down your dreams, to pay attention to the themes and symbols and your associations with them. Sometimes even words that *sound* like something else can be a hint at what your subconscious is telling you!

Author's Note

Now that we've gone through a bit of the background behind the history, philosophy, and science of dreaming, and now that you're armed with some tools to excavate your own subconscious, it's time to explore some of the symbols you might see in your sleep—and understand how your dreams are speaking to you.

As I wrote earlier, this project was born out of creative necessity. My artistic inspiration stems from my extremely vivid (and often lucid) dream world, and I love sharing how to unlock that process with others, often through art journaling or creative writing. The more I researched dream interpretation, the more fascinated I became with global, cultural, and historical connections to specific symbols and themes (for example, I did not know, prior to writing this book, that umbrellas are actually good luck symbols in Buddhism).

The intuitive portions of each dream come from my own connections between the symbols and thinking deeper as to what each could mean. I start from a place of critical thinking (as I would when critiquing a film or literature) and approach it as if dreams are works of art. And you'll find I do love a good pun or play on words. However, many of the intuitive connections are not wholly my original ideas, in that many dream experts and psychologists often arrive at the same conclusion (for example, dreaming of being naked is "exposing" yourself; crocodiles are literally "hidden dangers").

For deeper research on dream science and symbols, I started with a collection of classic resources by Adele Nozedar, Sigmund Freud, Carl Jung, J. E. Cirlot, and others. I then conducted more in-depth research using multiple websites, journals, and print reference materials.

For those who want to dive even deeper into dream exploration, the science and psychology behind it, and how to enhance your own lucid dreaming through practice and tools, flip to the back of the book, where you'll find a detailed list of resources.

I hope the following pages inspire you to explore deeper, learn more about yourself, and start seeing the world around you in a more connected way.

Pay attention to the themes and symbols and your associations with them. Sometimes even words that sound like something else can be a hint at what your subconscious is telling you!

Chapter 5

Symbols and Themes

Aliens

WAS IT AN ALIEN ABDUCTION . . . or just a dream? Think about your connection to the alien or aliens from your subconscious adventure. Do you gravitate (pun intended) toward the unexplained and delight in abduction stories? If so, this might be a dream come true! If not, think of your association with the word alien in waking life—that is, when you're not talking about beings from the far reaches of space. Is there something unfamiliar you are experiencing right now? It could be a new project, an upcoming trip, or simply feeling like you aren't fitting in. The alien's arrival shows you are not alone!

Describe the alien.

Could you communicate with it?

How did you feel?

Is there something new and unfamiliar in your waking life?

Apocalypse

DREAMING OF THE END OF THE WORLD, or surviving after it happens, is what nightmares (and Hollywood movies) are made of. Each religious belief has its own version of the end times, but all have an ultimate theme: judgment. Will you or won't you make the cut when the trumpet sounds?

These dreams, as anxiety-inducing as they can be, are often reminders that all good things must come to an end. This isn't always bad, though! Like dreams of death (page 65), apocalyptic dreams can happen when something massive has changed, or is about to change, in your life and something new is on the horizon. Take a good look at how you reacted during this dream (were you calm under pressure, or fearful and jittery?) and what tools you used to forge a path in a new and strange world (were you mentally unprepared, or flexible and inventive?). Life's big changes don't have to be the end of the world as you know it.

● Was this pre- or post-apocalypse? Or during?

● What was the biggest threat to you?

● What survival skills did you possess?

● What is coming to a close in your waking life?

Apples

APPLES HAVE BEEN THE CENTERPIECE of myth and folklore for thousands of years. A golden apple, representing discord and beauty, ultimately started the Trojan War in ancient Greece. When Eve bit into the apple from the tree of knowledge, she had an awakening. Snow White's apple bite led to a long slumber, with only true love's kiss to awaken her.

Because of these stories, apples have become symbols for knowledge, temptation, and immortality. The fruit itself is considered magical because of its cross section of seeds. When an apple is cut in half, the five seeds create a star shape, similar to a pentagram (a symbol for protection against evil).

As with many food dreams, consider what needs nourishment in your life. You may be craving deeper knowledge or something . . . sweeter.

- Did you eat the apple?
- What was the condition of the apple?
- Did someone give you the apple, or did you gift it to someone?
- What information are you seeking in your waking life?

Attacks

What if, when a violent intruder comes into your (dream) house at night, it's actually you? That was psychoanalyst Carl Jung's belief. He proposed that these mysterious "shadow" figures are repressed traits of our subconscious, and that when they arrive in dreams it is a safe way to engage with them and understand ourselves more. They often show up as monsters, unknown figures, or even as one's self.

Think about who your symbolic attacker was and what traits they had. Did the fight give you confidence that you could come out on top, or did it leave you even more scared? What are you fiercely protecting in waking life, and what feels under attack? Look at both sides of the fight, both in your dream and waking life, and see if you can find a middle ground.

Do note that if the dream is a recurring nightmare based on an attack you experienced in waking life, you may be suffering from PTSD and should consider seeking professional help.

See also Being Chased (page 41); Devil (page 67); Werewolf (page 151); Zombie (page 153).

- Were you attacking or being attacked?
- Who was on the other side of the fight?
- What was the outcome?
- What areas do you feel you are protecting or defending in your waking life?

Avalanche

MADE OF SNOW AND ICE, avalanches can come crashing down with devastating force and be initiated by the slightest trigger. When you dream of an avalanche, are you caught in the path, or did you initiate the destruction? Because water is an element tied to emotions and snow is a frozen version of water, your dream avalanche is very likely a symbol of cold emotions in your life. It can also mean that you've been repressing your emotions for so long that it's time for them to burst out. Think about how you can go with the flow safely. If the emotions belong to someone else, how can you move out of the way?

See also Mountains (page 108); Storms (page 134); Water (page 148).

- What caused the avalanche?
- Was anyone hurt?
- Were you in it or watching it?
- What is crashing down on you in your waking life right now?

Avocado

- Did you eat it?
- How fresh was the avocado?
- Who was with you in the dream?
- What fruitful areas of your waking life are bursting with potential?

THE AVOCADO IS A FRUIT WORTHY OF FREUDIAN ANALYSIS. It is a symbol of love and fertility and is said to be translated as "testicle" from the Aztec word *āhuacatl*. Full of monounsaturated fats and antioxidants, avocados are also good for the heart. A true aphrodisiac!

In nature, avocados dangle in pairs on a tree and have the botanical criteria of a berry. With tough, leathery skin and soft, creamy insides, the symbols and metaphors practically write themselves. They are truly symbols of good health, love, and fruitful ideas. Or maybe you're just really craving some avocado toast.

Babies

LIKE DREAMING OF BEING PREGNANT OR CHILDBIRTH, dreaming of a baby doesn't necessarily predict that you are going to have one soon. (Although if you are actually pregnant, dreaming of giving birth is a natural and common dream.) Rather, babies can represent something new, like an idea, a project, or a relationship.

There is a sense of innocence that also comes with babyhood. Like The Fool tarot card, it evokes playfulness, joy, and the beginning of a long journey ahead without much worry or planning (unless, of course, you are a parent, in which case worry takes on a whole new meaning).

Whatever this relates to in your life will need nurturing and care. It may take up a lot of energy, keep you up at night, and make you question your path and choices. Despite overwhelming emotion, this time can be extremely exciting, with potential for growth and adventure.

See also Eggs (page 72); Numbers (page 22); Pregnancy/Birth (page 116).

Whose baby was it?

What was the baby's demeanor?

What was your primary emotion?

What is something brand-new you are experiencing in waking life?

Balcony

BALCONIES CAN BE AN EXTENSION of your living space, providing a bigger view of the world around you. If you have a dream in which you are on a balcony, consider the building it was attached to and the support it provided. In dreams, Carl Jung believed that houses are representative of our bodies and souls. In this case, a dream balcony might help your subconscious gain more perspective.

Because of their elevated status, balconies also symbolize power and authority, and they have served as literal platforms for popes and politicians to deliver messages to the masses. In 1951, First Lady of Argentina Eva Perón spoke to a rally of two million from a balcony, and the event was immortalized in the musical *Evita*. The balcony scene in William Shakespeare's *Romeo and Juliet* has in and of itself become a collective symbol of longing and separation. Those sentiments are key to the lovers' short relationship; the balcony is a visual representation of those barriers.

But the balcony can also indicate vulnerability and visibility that may not be welcome: Someone hidden below might very well be able to hear or see what's going on up above.

See also House (page 89).

What could you see from your view on the balcony?

How sturdy was the balcony?

Was anyone looking up at you?

What in your waking life could use a new perspective?

Bathing

A BATH IS A PURIFICATION PROCESS, washing away the grime and dirt of the day. Immersing yourself in water can be a baptism, a ritual, or simply a luxurious way to care for yourself.

In Shakespeare's *Macbeth*, washing away blood signifies a guilty conscience, and while you may not have committed a crime so horrific as murder for political advancement, dreaming of bathing could hint at guilt or worry deep down in your subconscious mind.

Allow yourself to fully submerge in that dream tub and think about the situations surrounding your bath. Was the water murky? Did you feel refreshed and renewed after emerging from the tub? And what in your waking life is leaving you feeling, well . . . dirty?

See also Water (page 148).

- Where were you bathing?
- What was the water quality like?
- Is there something in your waking life that needs cleansing?
- What are you seeking in your spiritual life?

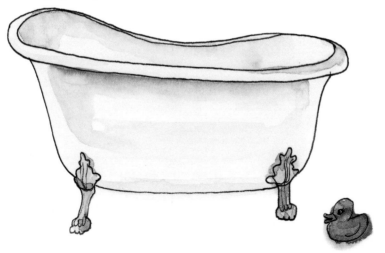

Bats

As a species, bats are quite fascinating! They are the only mammals that can fly for long periods and are the only flying animals that nurse their young. Bats aren't actually blind, but due to their nocturnal lifestyle, they have poor vision and use echolocation to identify their surroundings.

Despite negative connotations surrounding bats, in many cultures they are auspicious symbols; the Chinese pronunciation of "bat" is the same as "good fortune," and in Hinduism bats are linked with the goddess Lakshmi, bestower of wealth and beauty. Look at some of the components of your dream to figure out what the bat meant to you. Did the bat emerge out of darkness and into light? If so, consider that a symbol of birth or transition. Did the bat bite you like a vampire? Perhaps something—or someone—in waking life is draining you emotionally.

Also, consider that bats are nocturnal and are active mainly at night. Is there a dark side of your subconscious or personality that is coming out to play? How you interacted with the bat can give a hint to secrets you are unlocking.

Where was the bat?

Did it bite you?

How do you normally feel about bats?

What darkness are you emerging from in your waking life?

Being Chased

ONE OF THE MOST COMMON AND UNIVERSAL DREAMS, being chased can be a true nightmare. In it, you may find that your legs stop working, your voice is unable to call for help, or there are multiple obstacles in your path preventing you from a successful escape.

As with most anxiety dreams, dreams of being chased tend to be direct reflections of your waking life's stresses. Think carefully about who was chasing you. If it was a dark, shadowy figure or monster, consider that to be an element of yourself that you aren't ready to face. If that doesn't apply, think about areas in your life that you have neglected for too long that are now catching up to you. If this becomes a recurring dream, remember: It's just a dream! Turn around and face your fears, and see what happens when you fight back.

See also Devil (page 67); Werewolf (page 151); Zombie (page 153).

- Who was chasing you?
- What obstacles did you face?
- How close was your pursuer?
- What areas of life have you neglected that are finally catching up to you?

Birds

WHO OR WHAT HAS WINGS AND FEATHERS? Angels; Hermes, the Greek god of messengers; mythical creatures like Pegasus and griffons . . . and birds! As a class, birds have been closely connected with the spiritual and the divine, serving as messengers between heaven and earth. In dreams, birds may be bringing you messages from the beyond or serving as reminders of your potential, of who you can become.

Look at how the birds appeared in your dream and if they seemed to communicate with you. This could be an example of a visitation dream (page 16). Otherwise, where can you learn to soar to new heights? If you were the bird in the dream, use those wings, because it's time to fly.

Let's look closer at some birds that you may encounter in your dreams:

Crows & Ravens

FEW BIRDS EVOKE such mystery and prophecy as crows and ravens. Because of their deep, chattery voices, their "messages" have been symbolic components of myths and literature. Crows, along with foxes and rabbits, are often considered archetypal tricksters, possessing secrets or knowledge and disrupting social norms.

While many cultures see the crow as a positive symbol, because of a diet that includes carrion and the fact that a group of crows is called a "murder," these birds have also been associated with death and negative omens.

Owls

CLOSELY CONNECTED TO ATHENA, the Greek goddess of wisdom, owls have become a common symbol for knowledge. The physical features of owls contribute to their connection with wisdom: They are able to twist their necks almost in a full circle, giving them the gift of extended sight. Some owls, such as the great horned owl and the screech owl, are seen as evil omens in Cherokee lore. In part because of their nocturnal habits and because of their tufted "horns," these owls are linked with shape-shifters and witches.

Roosters

ROOSTERS LET US KNOW WHEN MORNING has arrived, making them symbols of the sun. From their strut and swagger come the words "cock" and "cocky." Roosters have something to say, and they demand you listen! They are one of the twelve symbols of the Chinese zodiac, and people born in the Year of the Rooster are said to be confident, communicative, and intelligent.

Swans

GRACEFUL AND BELONGING TO BOTH water and air, swans have attracted artists and poets for centuries. They symbolize faithfulness and fidelity, as they choose only one mate for life. They're particularly present in Greek mythology, where they are sacred to both Aphrodite, goddess of love and beauty, and Apollo, god of music and truth and the leader of the Muses. Though the idea that a swan sings sweetly before death is purely metaphorical, the phrase "swan song" is used to describe one's final performance, work, or accomplishment before retirement or death.

See also Feathers (page 77);
Flying (page 81).

- What kind of bird was it?
- Were you the bird?
- What was the bird doing?
- Who have you been wishing to communicate with in your waking life?

Books

FIRE MAY HAVE ADVANCED HUMANKIND to the next stage of evolution, but books sparked our brains into being. Books represent knowledge, even in a time and era when so much information can be found digitally. They can be spiritual manuals guiding entire religions and mythologies, a means to learn and discover the unknown, or simply a form of entertainment.

Think about the state of the book in your dream and whether it was open or closed. What knowledge are you keeping hidden, and what stories do you need to share?

Consider its genre and apply that to what you might be seeking more of in life. Were you reading a biography of someone you admire or escaping to another planet in a work of science fiction? Perhaps the bright colors and imaginative illustrations of a children's book will inspire you to be more playful in your waking life. And don't forget to heed the age-old advice: Don't judge a book by its cover!

- Were you reading or writing the book?
- What was the book about?
- How far into the book were you?
- Is there a story in your waking life that you need to tell?

Bread

CORNBREAD, biscuits, bagels, naan, tortillas, mantou, baguettes. . . . Are you hungry yet? A food staple, bread is a cultural identifier and has even been an object of social class. (White bread, because of its milling and refining process, was a marker of high society and extremely expensive. Today, refined white bread graces most grocery store shelves, and rustic whole-wheat artisanal loaves are the high-end product.) Bread also has spiritual significance in Christianity, where it symbolizes the body of Jesus. Therefore, eating bread in a dream can be considered a gift from God.

Because bread can be associated with livelihood and basic needs, it has also come to mean money, as in "I gotta earn that dough." In dreams, think about what you did with the bread. Did you offer it to others in a symbol of generosity? Did you feast on it yourself, symbolizing abundance in your life?

See also Food (page 82); Money (page 106).

● Where did you see the bread?

● Did you eat the bread, or did you share it?

● In what condition was the bread? Fresh and warm or moldy and stale?

● What is something in your waking life that is fulfilling?

Breaking Up

LET'S REVISIT DREAM SYMBOLISM 101: People in your dreams aren't always representations of the same person in your waking life. When your partner breaks up with you in a dream, it's not necessarily time to start questioning everything you've said and done over the last week. Dreaming of a breakup can be a message for you to look at some messy areas in your life, relationships included, and see what needs cleaning up.

Are you struggling with a creative project? Did you not get the job you wanted? Perhaps you've been dealing with some inner negative thoughts and self-esteem issues. Sweep up that shattered dream heart and glue it back together, making it stronger and more resilient against future blows.

See also People (page 20).

Who broke up with whom?

What feels broken in your waking life?

How did you feel about the breakup?

What is going on in your current relationships?

Bridges

AS AN ARCHITECTURAL STRUCTURE, bridges provide safe passage and support from one point to another, usually over an obstacle, such as water or a ravine. They allow us to go to places beyond our reach. As a concept, bridges can connect (or disconnect, if you choose to "burn bridges" with someone).

Symbolically, bridges represent connection, support, and transition. What part of your life needs a clear and easy path that may not be readily accessible? Perhaps there's someone in your life the bridge represents, whether as a support structure or the obstacle beneath it. In dreams, the presence of a bridge may also be a clue that you are traveling between your conscious and subconscious thoughts. What happened when (or if) you got to the other side? This dream can spark you into action, into bridging the gap between what you desire and actually achieving it.

In what condition was the bridge?

Were you able to get across?

What was on the other side of the bridge?

What are some obstacles you face in your waking life, and what support do you need?

Bubbles

BUBBLES CAN EVOKE PLAYFULNESS AND FUN. Think of how satisfying it was as a kid to blow that perfect soap bubble. And what better way to celebrate a special occasion than with an effervescent bottle of "bubbly"? When ideas bubble up to the surface, it's usually a very exciting time full of energy.

Yet bubbles are also fragile and fleeting, and they can represent a form of protection if you need sheltering. Bursting that bubble can crush your spirit, whether you do it yourself or someone does it for you. Look at your dream bubbles and examine what you are having fun with in your waking life and what needs extra protection, and remember to open your eyes to the world outside your shimmery sphere!

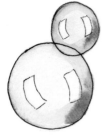

- How did the bubbles appear?
- Were you in a bubble?
- Did the bubble pop?
- What in your waking life needs protecting right now?

Bugs

IN WAKING LIFE, bugs aren't something you probably want crawling all over you. The faster you brush them off, the better, right? But when they show up in a dream, if you can, let them crawl and flutter. They show up for a reason.

Bugs go through stages of transformation throughout their relatively short lives. Because of this, they represent change, metamorphosis, and rebirth. In Ancient Egypt, scarabs—a type of beetle—were sacred. They were used as amulets to help safely deliver the deceased to the afterlife.

Depending on the bug, you might think about where it lives, what it eats, and how it transforms. Look at what is changing in your life, what might be bothering you, and how thick of a shell you have as protection. This is one of those symbols where wordplay can be a clue to interpreting your dream. Is something "bugging you"? Have you "caught a bug" (like a flu or virus)? Or are you "bugging out" with anxious thoughts? Remember to think metaphorically and abstractly about your dream critters.

See also Butterflies (page 50); Moth (page 107); Wasp (page 147).

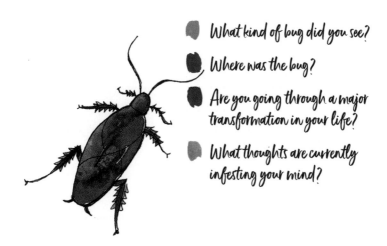

- What kind of bug did you see?
- Where was the bug?
- Are you going through a major transformation in your life?
- What thoughts are currently infesting your mind?

Butterflies

BUTTERFLIES ARE A POLLINATOR SPECIES and found across the globe. They are usually brightly colored and can migrate over great distances. Because of their very visible four-stage life cycle, which includes a massive transformation from caterpillar to butterfly, they are often symbols of rebirth, renewal, transformation, and metamorphosis.

In ancient Greek, the word for "butterfly," *psyche*, translates to "soul." Psyche, in mythology, was married to Cupid and was depicted with a pair of wings. Across cultures and history, butterflies have also been connected with spiritual communication. Like its cousin the moth, a butterfly can represent a message from a departed soul.

Think about your own creative and spiritual growth. What stage do you feel like you're in right now? Are you a cocooned caterpillar, or a newly minted butterfly?

- Did you see a butterfly, or were you one?
- What color (or colors) was it?
- How many butterflies did you see?
- What areas are in transition in your waking life?

Camera

THE CAMERA ITSELF has evolved significantly since its invention in the 1600s, and because of this, our subject matter has shifted. In its early years, the camera was used primarily for portraits immortalizing a person's image. Today, with immediate access to cameras, you can capture fleeting moments anytime, anywhere. Looking at photos triggers memories, and with them, a sense of nostalgia. (Or regret—evidence of outdated fashion trends will outlive us all!)

What lens are you looking through in your waking life? Is it time to refocus, look at a bigger picture, or hone in on a detail? If the photos were taken of you, consider who was behind the camera and how you felt as your photo was taken. A picture is worth a thousand words, so what story is your dream asking you to tell?

See also Mirror (page 105).

- Were you in front of or behind the camera?
- Who or what was the subject of the photograph?
- What needs to be in focus in your waking life?
- What moments are you wanting to remember?

Candle

LIKE A LIGHT BULB, a candle can symbolize ah-ha moments, where the darkness falls away and a path of action or an idea suddenly appears. It can also represent your conscious self finally understanding elements of your subconscious.

In many religions, candles are used for intention setting, like prayers and offerings. The smoke from an extinguished flame can be a communication tool with the spiritual realm, offering those prayers and (birthday) wishes to the world beyond.

Look at who lit that candle and what you were able to see once it was glowing. Conversely, did someone snuff out the flame, leaving you in darkness? Use your dream candle to think about your inner light and what it can do to the darkness around you.

See also Fire (page 79); Light Bulb (page 98).

Who lit the candle?

Did it get extinguished?

What did the candlelight expose?

Where do you need some illumination in your waking life?

Carrots

CONTRARY TO POPULAR OPINION, carrots do not actually help your night vision (though they are rich in Vitamin A, which is vital for general eye health). This was a myth created during World War II when the Royal Air Force wanted to keep their new radar technology a secret. They claimed their pilots had such great night vision because of . . . carrots.

Our acceptance of this myth, however, is deeply embedded in our knowledge bank. When a carrot shows up in your dream, think of it as a symbol of clear sight—you're perhaps becoming aware of something in your waking life. You'll need to be patient, though, because a carrot can take up to four months to grow from a seed before you can dig it out of the ground. And even though they don't scientifically improve your night vision, they are incredibly nourishing—just some extra food for thought.

See also Colors (page 24); Food (page 82).

- Did you eat a carrot?
- What was the state of the carrot? Raw, cooked, rotten?
- What (or who) is "rooted" in your life right now that is causing concern?
- What in your waking life needs some digging to obtain?

Cats

WHETHER YOU CONSIDER YOURSELF A CAT PERSON OR NOT, it's hard to deny that cats are magical, intuitive creatures. These fiercely independent animals have been adored for thousands of years, from the ancient Egyptian deity Bast to contemporary internet memes. They have long been associated with witchcraft and magic, leading to superstitions around black cats.

At the most basic level, cats symbolize a mysterious instinct and rebirth (nine lives, anyone?). Depending on whether you found a cat, lost a cat, or were a cat, think about areas in your waking life where you need to reconnect with your deep, intuitive spirit, independence, and inner power.

- Where did you see the cat?
- What was the cat's disposition?
- How independent do you feel?
- How do you connect to your intuitive side in your waking life?

CAVES ARE DEEP, DARK, AND FULL OF LIFE. They are unexpected places for amazing growth, but that growth can take a lot of time. If this is starting to sound like a womb, you've made an age-old symbolic connection. Because of this, caves are seen as a motherly archetype, nurturing deep intuitional knowledge and an opportunity for rebirth.

What happens when you emerge from a cave and are blinded by the light of the outside world? The Greek philosopher Plato talked about the cave as an unintentional prison—not until you escape can you discover what else exists in the world outside.

When a cave shows up in your dream, think about all the things you know and acknowledge how much you don't. What is holding you back from leaving your dream cave? What do you think you'll find upon exiting? And what areas in your waking life are ready for renewal, emergence, and rebirth?

- Did you enter or exit the cave?
- What was inside the cave?
- What tools did you have with you?
- What are you internalizing that might be ready to emerge?

Cheating

LIKE WITH A DREAM OF BREAKING UP WITH SOMEONE (page 46), just because you had an affair with someone in your dream does not necessarily mean you are an unfaithful partner, or vice versa. Rather, these dreams usually highlight our own insecurities and self-esteem issues. It can be a great time to talk with your partner and find out what they are insecure about, as well. Are you communicating in ways they appreciate? Do you feel like you aren't being valued enough in your own relationship?

Think about the person you were with in the dream or who your partner chose over you. What traits do they have that you admire? Do you feel you lack those in your own life? These dreams can be disheartening, but they're helpful in allowing us to take an honest look at what we are feeling low about.

If it was a test or competition you cheated on, what were the stakes if you lost? Look at those losses and how they affected your sense of self-worth through the eyes of your own insecurities in waking life.

- Who (or what) was being cheated on?
- Did you (or they) get caught?
- How did it make you feel?
- What areas in your waking life do you feel insecure about?

Climbing

CLIMBING IN A DREAM can be a straightforward symbol of your waking life aspirations. What sets this dream apart from, let's say, dreams of stairs or elevators is that the act of climbing is not passive. Climbing takes all of your energy and courage. And depending on what tools you had with you in the dream, a mistake could lead to falling (page 76).

If you have set some lofty goals for yourself, use this dream as a reminder to pack all the necessary tools and build the stamina it will take for the process. Exciting times are in front of you, but only if you plan ahead!

- What were you climbing?
- How high up did you get?
- What obstacles did you face?
- What goals are you working toward in your waking life?

Conch Shell

WHO HASN'T HELD A CONCH SHELL up to their ear to try to hear the ocean? Buddhists believe that sound represents the "Om," a sound of cosmic law and order. Hearing it awakens those who may be in a deep slumber of ignorance, and it is the sacred emblem of the Hindu god Vishnu. The conch has been used as a symbol of trumpeting, such as in William Golding's *Lord of the Flies*, in which the shell announced group meetings and gave the holder permission to speak (until it didn't . . .).

The shell itself can house a variety of sea snails, and its spiral shape symbolizes infinity. It belongs to water (page 148), which has its own set of symbols, including birth, fertility, and transcendence from earthly to heavenly. With so many elements at its core, think about what you need to listen to or, conversely, what needs to be heard.

Where did you find the conch shell?

What condition was it in?

What did you do with the shell?

What part of you needs to be heard right now?

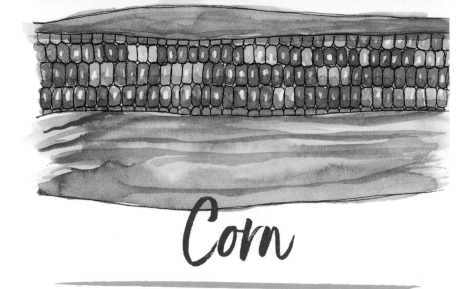

Corn

CORN IS A NATURAL SYMBOL OF FERTILITY AND ABUNDANCE, with each ear of corn containing around eight hundred seeds. It is part of the "three sisters" foods that sustained Indigenous people of the Americas for thousands of years, alongside beans and squash. Each tribe has its own powerful creation story, such as that of the Corn Mother.

The Corn Mother is a mythological figure in Indigenous folklore, but every version of her story includes a common theme of sacrifice and love. Selu, the Cherokee's Corn Mother, supported her family by creating new corn through rubbing her body. Once found out by her sons, she grew ill and died, but not before leaving instructions on how to prepare her body to keep the corn growing. Through this continual growing of the corn, she attained eternal life.

In the Christian bible, corn plays an important role in dream interpretation: Joseph dreams of corn stalks bowing down to him, and when he tells the tale, his brothers sell him into slavery. Later the Pharaoh dreams of seven heads of healthy grain, followed by seven withered heads. Through God, Joseph interprets this dream to mean that Egypt will experience seven years of abundance followed by seven years of hardship. This allows the Egyptians to plan ahead and weather the famine.

What is abundant in your life? How can you help others with this surplus?

Where was the corn growing?

What form did the corn take? Fresh, dried, popped?

Did you eat the corn?

What do you have an abundance of in your waking life?

Crash

ACCIDENTS HAPPEN, but being in a serious crash—car, boat, bicycle, motorcycle, or airplane—can be extremely traumatic. In waking life, it usually means someone was out of control or negligent and likely caused injury to someone or something. When dreaming of a crash, think about what you are losing control over in waking life. Often these accidents happen in the blink of an eye, with little time to prepare. The driver's carelessness could mean someone else's (symbolic) injury. Were you the driver?

Use this dream as a reminder to be present and alert and to keep a firm grip on the wheel of life! If you were a passenger, think about how you felt and what control you lacked. It might be time to become a more active participant by taking over in the driver's seat and heading in a direction *you* choose.

See also Transportation (page 143).

How did the crash happen?

What injuries did you sustain?

Could you see it coming?

What issues in your waking life are you having trouble controlling?

Crocodiles and Alligators

THESE PREHISTORIC REPTILES are known for their tough skin, powerful strength, and ability to remain hidden until they suddenly strike their prey. As such, the appearance of a crocodile or alligator can remind you to toughen up, be still, and act when the time is right.

The ancient Egyptian deity Sobek featured a crocodile head on a man's body. Egyptians would pray to him for protection from the dangers of the Nile as well as for fertile crops. Crocodiles were such a prominent part of the culture that they were kept in temples, adorned with jewels, and mummified.

A crocodile is not an animal many people welcome in the wild. When one shows up in your dream, it may be suggesting a hidden danger. If you are the crocodile, think about something in your waking life that you are sensitive about. And though crocodiles and alligators do have minor differences, the symbolism rings true for both.

Were you the crocodile?

Did it bite you?

Was it on land or in water?

What is something in your waking life that you need thicker skin to deal with?

Crystals

CRYSTALS HAVE BEEN USED for thousands of years as decoration, protection, and healing. Ancient Egyptians placed gemstones on bodies during mummification to protect the deceased in the afterlife. In Ayurvedic medicine, the use of different gemstones is said to help balance our doshas, or energies in the body.

Even if you can't tell jade from jasper, when a crystal or gemstone shows up in your dream, consider the following: color, shape, and its state (was it raw and from the earth, or polished to perfection on a piece of jewelry?). Then think about which areas in your life are muddled, which areas are "crystal" clear, and where you might need some guidance. Using crystals is a fun way to set your intentions and be reminded of them when you see the shiny pieces of earth on your desk or by your bed.

Here are some of the most popular crystals and the themes they represent in your dreams:

AMETHYST: A great crystal for dreamwork, it is said to relieve nightmares and insomnia. Other uses include promoting sobriety, balance, and aiding in clear vision.

CITRINE: Lemony yellow in color (*citron* is French for "lemon"), this powerful crystal is associated with the sun, abundance, and manifestation.

FLUORITE: A favorite crystal to use when you need some organization in your life! It's said to absorb negative energy and help with grounding and improving self-confidence.

MALACHITE: A stunning blue and green crystal containing copper, it is used to absorb negative energy, protect against the evil eye, and open your heart to unconditional love.

MOONSTONE: When activated during a full moon, this reflective crystal can enhance lucid dreaming.

QUARTZ: The most common crystal, it comes in dozens of color variations and is used to amplify your intentions. True crystal balls are made from polished quartz.

RED JASPER: Part of the quartz family, it absorbs negative energy and aids in calming emotions. It's a great crystal for promoting dream recall.

If you want to add crystals to your dreamwork, see page 12 for instructions on how to create a pouch to keep under your pillow.

What kind of crystal or stone was it?

Where did you find the crystal?

How did you use it?

Where are you seeking clarity in your waking life?

Darkness

DARKNESS IS MYSTERIOUS, menacing, and frightening. It's a natural representation of the night, and in movies and literature it's a common symbol of evil. When darkness shows up, it can be scary. According to Carl Jung, though, darkness is essential for us to be well-rounded human beings. If we're all good or all evil, where is the balance? Finding light in the dark and dark in the light is a crucial tool we all can benefit from, and it's a powerful coping mechanism for when times get tough.

Look at how you felt about and responded to the darkness in your dream. In what areas of your waking life have you felt the same emotions? How can you add some extra light, happiness, joy, or silliness to those feelings and situations?

- How did the darkness present itself?

- Was anyone (or anything) with you?

- Did you ever find light?

- What are you currently having difficulty dealing with?

Death

DEATH DREAMS CAN BE SCARY, emotional, and nightmarish. You might wake up in a panic, wondering if it's an omen or a premonition. Chances are—hopefully—that's not the case. In fact, dreaming of death can be an optimistic message. It serves as a symbolic reminder that all things, good or bad, must end.

Take tarot cards. The Death card represents an ending, and with it, a transition and a new beginning. It is connected with the number thirteen, which is either extremely unlucky (think Friday the 13th) or a number of leadership and success (King Arthur and his twelve knights, for one).

Which of your projects, jobs, or relationships are in their final days? What would happen if you decided to "pull the plug" on something that's not going anywhere for you? As the saying goes, when one door closes, another one opens.

● Who died, and how?

● What role did you play in the death?

● How did you feel about the death?

● What feels like it is coming to a close in your waking life?

Deer

THE GENTLE, swift deer is a mystical, divine communicator. In mythology deer are often golden or have gold antlers. They are associated with the Greek goddess of the hunt, Artemis. In Hinduism, deer are connected to the goddess of learning, Saraswati.

Did your dream deer have antlers? Antlers are an extension of the crown, tying back to knowledge and learning, but also reaching toward the heavens. Deer are often hunted for the trophies of their antlers, which are also used in decorations and alternative medicine. Shamans across cultures wear antlers as headdresses in hopes of communicating with the spiritual realm.

Because of the deer's spiritual connection, they are part of the group of animals known as psychopomps (page 21). In line with Jung's belief that wild animals are representative of our instincts and self, think about how you communicated with the dream deer and what it might have been trying to say. More importantly, what divine source could be sending you these messages?

● Where did you see the deer?

● What was the deer doing?

● How did it make you feel?

● What instincts have you acted upon lately?

Devil

IF YOU'RE GOING TO PLAY WITH FIRE, prepare to be burned! The devil has many names: Baphomet, Demogorgon, Lucifer, and Satan, just to name a few. Devils are tricksters, manipulators, and a universal symbol of evil. But they also have a lot of fun being that way! They are a concept as old as time and seen across cultures, predating the Christian Devil, and are often depicted with horns, cloven feet, and a human body.

Just because you dream of devils, demons, or hell doesn't mean you are crossing over to the dark side. Your subconscious brain might be reminding you about some dark elements in your life related directly to you or to someone (or something) else. When a devil shows up, acknowledge that mischief and mayhem are normal and think about how you can bring light to balance out the dark.

See also Werewolf (page 151).

- How did the devil appear?
- What was the devil doing?
- Were you scared? Or confident?
- What kind of struggle did you have with the devil?

Dogs

LOYAL BEYOND MEASURE, dogs have been humans' companions for over six thousand years. As such, they represent protection and friendship. Dogs are also hard workers, guiding and guarding, hunting and shepherding.

Because of their keen sense of smell, dogs are considered messengers between the physical and spiritual worlds. Large black dogs are considered more ominous, however, and in folklore are seen as harbingers of death protecting the gates of the underworld.

Think about your attitude toward and connection with dogs in waking life and how they compare with the dog in your dreams. If the dog felt dangerous, look closely at where your loyalties lie. Is something causing you to shift your mindset? If the dog was happy and friendly, enjoy the company!

See also Animals (page 21).

- What disposition did the dog have?
- What was the dog doing?
- Did you recognize the dog?
- Are your loyalties in the right place?

Dolls

YES, DOLLS ARE AN INTEGRAL PART OF CHILDHOOD, and they're one way children learn through imaginary play and pretend. But they are also the basis of many a nightmare (and horror movie) and can elicit a genuine fear known as "pediophobia."

Different dolls can symbolize different themes in your dream. For example, a nesting doll might be a direct reflection on the internal layers of your personality. A rag doll could represent your limp feelings toward life. Effigies and dolls made to look like someone specific are common in religious ceremonies and folk magic and can add an element of mystery to your dreams.

Look at the condition of the doll and how it appeared in your dream. If dolls are truly symbolic of our childhood play, think about the current state of your inner child. Does it come out to play, or is it stuffed away and forgotten?

- What kind of doll was it?
- Whose doll was it?
- How did you interact with it?
- How do you connect with your inner child?

Dolphins

WHEN A DOLPHIN SHOWS UP IN YOUR DREAM, it usually means it's there to help. Just look at its happy, smiling face! These extremely intelligent mammals are found in oceans, and some rivers, all over the globe. They communicate with one another through sound and touch and use echolocation to find food and avoid predators.

Although they are air-breathing mammals, dolphins are able to exist underwater, making them a symbol of transition between worlds. Because of this, in Greek mythology, dolphins were seen as caring beings who escorted the recently deceased from earth to the afterlife.

Think about what you need extra help with and whether you're having trouble asking for that help. Dolphins, as intelligent communicators, are here to assist you. Their traits are meant to inspire you through life's challenges and changes and help you learn to be comfortable with discomfort.

- Where did the dolphin appear?

- How did you interact with the dolphin?

- What are some areas in your waking life where you are having trouble communicating to others using words?

- What is something you need extra help with?

Doors

THINK OF SOME OF THE MOST MAGICAL DOORS in literature and the worlds on the other side of them: Wonderland in *Alice in Wonderland*; the hidden garden in *The Secret Garden*; and the hope for safety in Mohsin Hamid's 2017 novel *Exit West*.

Doors symbolize portals to new worlds, new adventures, and new ideas. When a door shows up in your dream, you are being invited to explore! What you find on the other side may not be exactly what you hoped for, though. This is a time when you might start feeling more in tune with yourself and start noticing bigger connections with the world around you. If the door was heavy, hard to open, or locked, keep trying. You'll soon find the key that fits!

See also Keys (page 95).

- What did the door look like?
- Was it easy to open?
- Where did it lead?
- What have been "key" ah-ha moments for you lately?

Eggs

BECAUSE AN EGG IS A VESSEL from which life is born, it is often used to represent fertility, birth, and rebirth. The world or cosmic egg origin story is found in many mythologies: Once the "world egg" cracked open, its inner fluids became the heavens and earth, and gods and goddesses emerged.

When you look at an egg as a symbol of creation and beginning, consider that it can also be about incubating an idea. You can give birth to endless creative possibilities! We don't always have to take our dream symbols at face value, and an egg is a perfect example of that.

- Was the egg whole or cracked?

- What was inside? Raw yolk, a baby chick, or something else entirely?

- Do you have an idea or project you are thinking about starting?

- Is there something that needs protecting in your waking life?

Elevator

SIMILAR TO LADDERS AND STAIRS (page 133) and roller coasters (page 120), the elevator rising and falling can be a metaphor for your emotions, your aspirational or spiritual goals, or your physical health. What sets the elevator apart from the other ascension tools is that you are in an enclosed space with relatively little immediate control. If all goes well, you press a button, wait a few seconds, and arrive at your destination without having to expend much physical energy.

Based on Jung and Freud's theory that dream buildings and houses are a reflection of our body and mind, think about what physical and emotional ups and downs you are experiencing in waking life and how in control you are of them. Did someone push all the buttons before you stepped in? Were you trapped and frantic, or did you get where you needed to go? What happened when you stepped out of the doors? Figuring out some of these answers will help you lean back and enjoy the ride.

- Who was in the elevator with you?

- Were you going up or down?

- How did you feel in the elevator?

- What areas of your waking life are in a state of flux that you can't control?

Explosions

EXPLOSIVE BEHAVIOR CAN MANIFEST IN DREAMS as erupting volcanoes, bombs going off, or unknown catastrophes in the distance. How much you had a hand in the explosion can be a clue to how close you may be in your waking life to losing your cool. Use this dream as a safe way to step back and take a deep breath before something destructive happens. It's a sign that, in your waking life, you should take a closer look at your strongest emotions and explore them in a healthy way. If you were witnessing explosions, think about who or what in your life feels volatile and what you can do to defuse the situation.

See also Apocalypse (page 32); Fire (page 79).

- Where was the explosion?
- Was anyone injured or hurt?
- How close were you to the explosion?
- What are you bottling up and perhaps struggling to keep in?

Eyes

OUR EYEBALLS ASSIST IN OUTWARD VISION, working with our brain and (emotional) heart to process the information we see. Making direct eye contact with someone can trigger a belly flop of emotions, and inaction by pretending not to see something can be harmful.

Spiritually, an eyeball symbolizes God and the universe. Many Eastern religions describe an invisible "third eye" on the forehead, a center of enlightenment and a way to see beyond what our physical eyes are capable of seeing. Eyes are thought of as gateways to the soul and are used in symbolism across all cultures as forms of all-knowing, protection (like the evil eye), and truth.

Think about how the eyes appeared in your dream. Did you see a reflection of your own peepers, or did you get lost in the gaze of a loved one? When you say the word "eye" out loud, consider how it abstractly could mean "I" in your dreams. It very well might be time for some self-reflection.

- Whose eyes did you see?
- Did you make direct eye contact?
- What is catching your eye in your waking life?
- Where can you use a fresh pair of eyes for a problem?

Falling

FALLING DREAMS are one of the most common anxiety dreams, right up there with being chased (page 41) and teeth crumbling or falling out (page 139). There is a strong theme of losing control and losing it fast, with no time to course correct. Although the rules of gravity don't always apply in dreams, your fall may still be a frightful and unpleasant experience. Did you make it to the bottom? Or did you jolt awake before impact? In a physical sense, your dream fall might be so jarring that it abruptly awakens you. There's a reason for this: Falling dreams tend to happen at the beginning of our sleep cycles. Our bodies relax at this time, but sometimes we experience "hypnic jerks," or involuntary muscle contractions. Your brain signals you to awaken with a jolt.

In your waking life, are you falling fast and hard for someone? Are you overwhelmed? Maybe you feel like everything is falling apart in one or more areas of your life. Take this dream as a sign to pause, examine your fears, and discover where you can reclaim power.

● How fast were you falling?

● And from what height?

● Did you land?

● What areas in your waking life feel like they are falling apart?

Feathers

A POWERFUL SYMBOL OF HONOR AND RESPECT in many Indigenous communities, the feather is also associated with celestial symbolism and spiritual communication. When attached to a bird, feathers help give flight. The Greek god Hermes added feathers to his feet for swift movement. They are used to stabilize arrows in flight and as fans to help carry smoke during ceremonial smudging rituals. And let's not forget how a feather's quill became a mighty weapon of communication: the pen.

Keep in mind the color of your dream feathers, as colors can contain deeper meaning (page 24); it's said that white feathers are direct messages from angels. Feathers from different birds can also contain hidden symbolism (page 42). Even the function of the feather can be a specific message: Symmetrical feathers, often found on flightless birds like ostriches, represent truth and balance. Some feathers are meant for pure show to attract a mate, like the peacock's; others are soft and fluffy to protect against the cold.

Dreaming of feathers can communicate a lightness you need when you are on a path toward ascension. Whether it's a spiritual, professional, or physical journey, the feathers will assist you!

- What kind of feather was it?
- Where did you find it?
- What did you do with it?
- Where can you lighten up in your waking life?

Feet

THINK OF NEIL ARMSTRONG'S first footstep on the moon and its iconic impression. Leaving footprints shows you exist, that you have firmly planted yourself on this planet. They're a symbol of grounding, of stability.

Our feet are also powerful connectors to the rest of our physical body. Practitioners of reflexology, a form of healing dating back thousands of years, believe that the nerves from the bottom of our soles directly relate to other parts of our body. Through foot massage, reflexologists aid healthy blood and energy flow to our organs and promote general wellness.

In dreams, remember to consider word play. What condition are the soles in? If dreams connect us to our deeper self, use this as a reminder to look at the condition of your own soul. What needs grounding . . . or just a cozy pair of socks?

● Where were they taking you?

● What were they standing on?

● Were you wearing shoes? If so, what kind were they?

● What areas in your waking life could use some grounding?

Fire

FIRE IS NECESSARY TO HUMAN LIFE but dangerous when uncontrolled. It often describes someone's spirit and passion, as it is an intense and constantly moving element. Fire is and has been used in myriad religious ceremonies, whether as an offering to the gods, used in sacrifice, or lit as prayer intentions. Fire can be an agent of destruction, but out of its ashes something new can arise. It has the ability to help something transform and change shape.

Fire is rich in symbolism: It can indicate passion, lack of control, anger, transformation, purification, heat, or illumination. Consider the details of the fire. Did it keep you warm and cozy at home? Or was it out of control and harmful? Look at the people and emotions in your life. Is there someone or something that needs a bit of cooling off? Or, alternatively, is your life lacking energy and in need of a spark of passion?

See also Candle (page 52).

- What started the fire?
- Was the fire contained safely in a cozy hearth or uncontrolled in the wild?
- Did anyone or anything get burned?
- What is something that is getting out of control in your waking life? Does it need to be extinguished?

Fish

BECAUSE OF THEIR CONNECTION TO WATER (page 148), Jung believed that fish are messengers from our unconscious brain. A variety of cultures have theories as to what those messages might be: In China, the word for "fish" sounds very similar to the word for "abundance," so they are considered elements of good fortune. The ichthus, a symbolic representation of a fish, was a symbol early Christians used to identify themselves. In astrology, Pisces are known to be empathetic, creative, and emotional. Because fish can lay hundreds of eggs at a time, they are also a symbol of fertility.

What are you seeking in your waking life, and how close are you to catching it? If fish represent abundance, what tools do you need to set yourself up for success? This is also one of those dreams in which you'll want to pay attention to the color (goldfish—or gold fish—can represent your financial abundance, for example), the size, and the number of fish.

Think, too, about the fish's habitat in the dream. Was it swimming freely in the ocean or on display in a tiny glass bowl? If the fish was struggling for life out of water, compare that to how you feel right now. Are you experiencing new, uncomfortable situations? Overall, dreaming of fish is a great reminder to reflect on your own prosperity and abundance and to not let them slip through your fingers.

- What kind of water was the fish in?
- How many fish were there?
- How did you interact with the fish?
- What is something you're trying to "catch" in your waking life?

Flying

CREATURES WITH WINGS, such as birds and angels, represent a connection between the heavens and earth. Flying high above the ground, they are believed to deliver divine messages, and they symbolize peace and freedom.

In waking life, gravity keeps us literally grounded. When you dream of flying, you are free! You're also awarded a higher vantage point over the world and over your life. Think of what you aspire to. These goals could be professional, creative, or spiritual. What limitations prevent you from achieving them, and how does the world look from your new dream-flight perspective?

See also Birds (page 42); Feathers (page 77); Transportation (page 143).

- Was anyone with you, or were you flying solo?

- How high did you fly?

- How did you feel while flying? Excited, calm, anxious?

- What limitations are you feeling in your waking life?

Food

In addition to being one of our basic needs, food is an important part of rituals, religious ceremonies, gatherings, and even how we woo a potential lover. Because of its integral relationship to our well-being, food is also spoken of in terms of monetary value ("bringing home the bacon" and "that's my bread and butter"). We use it as a reward system (think "treats" and "comfort food") and often have fraught relationships with it involving control, or a lack thereof.

What kind of food did you see or eat in your dream, and what nourishing properties did it contain? Take into consideration your own relationship with food. Was your dream meal one that brought you joy or stress? Food can also indicate consumption of something else: knowledge, information, experiences. What do you need to feed yourself now?

See also Apples (page 33); Avocado (page 36); Bread (page 45); Carrots (page 53); Eggs (page 72); Fish (page 80); Salt (page 123).

What type of food did you see or eat?

What condition was it in?

How did it taste?

What needs nourishment in your waking life? What are you hungry for?

Garbage

TAKING OUT THE TRASH is getting rid of garbage, waste, and broken bits of things we no longer need. Trash can be evidence of a great time, like a roaring party or the unwrapping of gifts, but keeping it around will only cause clutter.

When garbage shows up in dreams, think about what emotions, relationships, or projects are not serving you. If they are stinking up your real or metaphorical house (page 89), it's time to reuse, recycle, or simply throw out.

Consider how you are treating your physical self. Are you eating processed food that is making you feel sluggish? And think about your mental self—maybe you're scrolling through toxic social media feeds or listening to pernicious gossip. Your subconscious brain might be begging you to clean up a bit!

Where was the garbage?

Was it your trash?

What did you do with it?

What do you no longer need in your waking life?

Ghosts

THE SUPERNATURAL WORLD IS UNKNOWN, intangible, and mysterious. When ghosts show up in your dreams, they can be scary or comforting. Because of their leading roles in many horror films, it's easy to immediately think they are omens of death or bad news. But some people aren't afraid—they actively invite them into their lives. On the Día de Muertos (Day of the Dead) in Mexico, people celebrate their deceased loved ones and hope for a visit from beyond. The dearly departed are gifted with altars, food, and flowers in a festive two-day celebration that takes an entire year of planning. If the living have done their job well, the dead will hear these messages and visit their friends and family, sometimes through dreams.

What was your dream spirit trying to communicate to you? Was it someone you knew, or an extension of yourself? It may have been a special visit from someone in your life asking for help or providing you with information from beyond your capabilities, or it may simply be a sign that you are haunted by the ghosts of your past. Pay attention to feelings of guilt, fear, or regret.

See also Invisibility (page 92); Nightmares (page 19); Visitation Dreams (page 16).

● How did the ghost appear?

● What did it try to communicate?

● How did you feel when you saw the ghost?

● What physical senses have you been disengaged with?

Giraffe

THERE ARE MANY "TALL TALES" surrounding the giraffe's unique physique, like it eating too many magical herbs or reaching its neck up to the heavens to greet its creator. Thousands of years ago, when the Sahara Desert was lush and green, prehistoric cultures carved life-size images of giraffes into rocks with intimate accuracy. One of the most famous carvings, in Niger, includes what looks to be a collar and leash around the giraffe's neck, suggesting they were held captive. Giraffes served as status symbols and pets centuries ago and were given as opulent gifts to Roman emperors.

Think about the perspective that giraffes have when one shows up in your dream. With their heads above the trees, they can see movement from up to a mile away. Are you currently taking a risk on something in waking life and need a new perspective? Or do you want to stand out above the crowd? Maybe it's time for *you* to stick your neck out.

- Where did you see the giraffe?
- Were you the giraffe?
- Was the giraffe in captivity or in the wild?
- Are you taking a big risk with something in your waking life?

Glass House

IF, ACCORDING TO JUNG, the house is a symbol of your body and soul, what does it being made of glass mean? Glass can be fragile and transparent, leaving you—inside the home—exposed.

Being on display can make you question your actions and behaviors, but sometimes not before the damage has already been done. Like the idiom "People who live in glass houses shouldn't throw stones," let this dream house remind you to be careful about criticizing others and to be conscious of thinking before speaking or acting.

Also consider the simple act of feeling exposed. What in your private life is on display for the world to see? Or are you trying desperately to hide something that needs to be seen?

● Was someone observing you?

● Whose house was it?

● Did the house protect you?

● What feels on display in your waking life?

Hair

HAIR IS A POWERFUL AND OBVIOUS IDENTIFIER of our culture, personality, and independence. Certain styles can be part of a uniform, like a ballerina's bun or a naval officer's cropped cut. They can be forms of rebellion, like the flowing locks of hippies. Baldness can represent religious commitments, like the shaved heads of Buddhist monks. Hair is also tied to vitality and life force, both symbolically and scientifically. Hair follicles can be tested for DNA, and our hair's physical properties can be clues about our health.

By creating your own hairstyle, you are harnessing the myriad nuances in meaning this symbol has. When you leave it in someone else's hands, you are offering a huge act of trust! Cutting someone's hair against their will has been used as a form of punishment and degradation.

Dreaming of hair, whether you lose it naturally, have it cut, or embrace its wild, untamed glory, is a reminder to look at what areas of life you have control of. If in your dream you're cutting your hair or changing the style you wear it in, consider any changes or shifts in your waking life. What purpose did the hair serve, and how did you feel about it?

What was the hairstyle?

Did you or someone else cut or lose it?

What were your emotions surrounding the hair?

What control is shifting in your waking life?

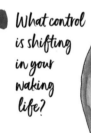

Hats

FEDORAS, FEZZES, FASCINATORS . . . hats are more than an ornamental piece of fashion. Throughout history they have served as identifiers for status (top hats), interests (sports teams), occupations (hard hats), and cultural heritage (what country do you think of when you see a beret?). They protect your head and face from the elements—or the paparazzi. Seeing a hat on someone can evoke an immediate response, whether it be of admiration or loathing. Donning a hat can make you feel more like yourself or allow you to try on a different role. Think about how you show up in the world and how you wish to appear to others.

Consider the context in which you wore or saw the hat, what kind it was, and how you felt about it. Because hats belong on the head—the source of intellect and the place where ideas are sparked and creativity is born—keep that part of your body in mind.

- What kind of hat was it?
- Did you put it on? How did you feel in it?

- Do you have a big idea that needs protecting?
- What current roles do you embody in your waking life?

House

HOUSES AS DREAM SYMBOLS are complex and worthy of deeper investigation. Both Freud and Jung believed that in dreams, a house symbolizes your body, and, even further, the home of your soul. Different parts of the house relate to different areas of your body and consciousness.

Were you in an attic? That could be your brain, the center of enlightenment. Did you submerge into a basement? Consider that the depths of your subconscious. Perhaps in your house you feel nurtured and cozy. That can symbolize a contented emotional heart.

A house, especially a *home*, shelters you and protects you from the outside elements. It can be a place of refuge, comfort, and self-expression. It can be a grand mansion or a simple tent. You've probably heard the phrase "your body is a temple." Think about how the house appeared in your dream and what cobwebs you might need to clear away, junk you might need to declutter, and prized possessions you might need to showcase.

See also Balcony (page 38); Doors (page 71); Elevator (page 73); Glass House (page 86); Secret Rooms (page 125); Stairs (page 133); Windows (page 152).

● What was the condition of the house?

● What rooms did you go in?

● How did you feel in the house?

● How is your body—your temple—feeling right now?

Hunting

DURING THE MIDDLE AGES the hunting of animals was a noble sport, helping the hunters show off military prowess and worthiness of the king's land and rule. Hunting has a strict set of rules, regardless of social class and era, and is highly regulated in several countries.

Hunting in a dream can easily symbolize something you are chasing after in waking life or an aspiration you wish to reach. Whether it's a romantic conquest or career goal, use this dream to figure out what tools you need to successfully track down what you are seeking. How can you develop confidence and empower yourself? And do you need this for survival or for bragging rights?

See also Being Chased (page 41); Deer (page 66); Trapped (page 144).

Who was the hunter? Was it you?

What were they hunting?

Did they succeed?

What are you seeking in your waking life?

Illness

MENTAL HEALTH can affect our dream state in many ways. When our mind is stressed, it affects our sleep patterns. In turn, disrupted sleep can provoke anxiety and depression, whether or not the person already experiences one or both of these conditions.

But what about physical health? Having a fever or being sick in your waking life can also affect your dreams, sometimes triggering nightmares. These "fever dreams" occur because your higher body temperature can disrupt sleep, including REM cycles. Interestingly, a study conducted in 2013 showed that people experiencing fever dreams had a common thread of burning or heat-related imagery.

During the early days of the COVID-19 pandemic in 2020, many people reported vivid and intense dreams. Due in part to heightened anxiety, the phenomenon of "COVID dreams" sparked interest across the globe. Psychologist Deirdre Barrett, who studies dreams during times of crisis, found that many metaphorical themes, such as bugs (page 49) and natural disasters (page 134), stood in place of the virus itself in dreams.

If your dream contained someone suffering from any type of illness—or if the patient was you—think about how different emotions affect you physically and see if that corresponds with the dream illness. Do you feel a burning pit in your stomach when you feel guilty or nervous? Or a tension headache when you are stressed? Carefully consider who around you in your dream was sick, the emotions you felt, and what role you played in their healing process. Were you Nurse Nightingale, or were you impatient and lacking bedside manner? Dreaming of sickness can be a reminder to look at your coping mechanisms and see what needs mending.

See also Medicine (page 104).

● Who was ill? Was it you?

● What part of the body was affected?

● How was the illness healed?

● What areas need nursing in your waking life?

Invisibility

HAVE YOU EVER THOUGHT ABOUT what you would do if you had the power of invisibility? When you control the power, there's an element of excitement and adventure.

Dreaming of invisibility serves as a reminder that there is more than meets the eye in our world, as well as in you. Think about how you became invisible and what you were doing with this new skill set. If in your dream you found yourself invisible without being able to control it, you may have experienced stress or alarm. Were you seeking help and nobody could hear or see you?

Look at what you are wanting acknowledgment for in your waking life. Are people noticing you or turning a blind eye? Do you feel undervalued? Don't give up! If the struggle continues, take advantage of your invisibility to get people questioning who is upending their world. These types of dreams will give you the superpower to make people finally see you.

See also Ghosts (page 84).

Were you invisible, or was someone else?

What were you doing while invisible?

Did you choose to be invisible?

In what areas of your waking life are you struggling to get noticed?

Jail/Imprisonment

THERE IS A COMMON THREAD that runs through dreams of being imprisoned: being locked away because of a criminal action you did—or didn't—do. What were those crimes in your dream, and how could they symbolically relate to something you're going through in your waking life?

Think about the emotional relationships in your life: partnerships, work, family. Are you feeling confined or wronged in any way? How can you free yourself from these emotions? Perhaps you were a family member or friend of the prisoner and feeling helpless. In that case, think about what assistance you can provide.

In the United States, over two million people are imprisoned or jailed each year, more than in any other country; it's a staggering social crisis that disproportionately hurts people of color and people who live in poverty. Having nightmares and other symptoms of PTSD is common for people who have been incarcerated. If you are suffering from PTSD, seeking professional help can be beneficial.

See also Trapped (page 144).

- Who was in jail?
- What caused the imprisonment?
- Did the prisoner ever get released?
- Where in your waking life are you feeling restricted or trapped?

Jewelry

JEWELRY CAN BE MORE THAN A FANCY ADORNMENT. Take, for example, the wedding ring. A ring worn on the left hand is most often an immediate cue of someone's relationship status, with the quality of the ring and stone an indicator of wealth (or credit card debt). The ancient Romans believed that our left finger contained a vein that led directly to the heart and that binding it with a ring was a lover's symbolic way of holding it tight.

Necklaces made of certain stones can serve as amulets and protection, and wearing a particular necklace can show others your religious beliefs (for example, a cross, Star of David, or Hamsa of Fatima). In the Western world, body piercing tends to be viewed as a symbol of rebellion, but it can also have cultural and religious connotations. In the Indian tradition of Ayurveda, piercing a woman's left nostril is said to enhance fertility.

Whether it's a family heirloom or a gifted charm bracelet, jewelry holds a monetary and emotional value. In dreams, dripping with jewels can indicate prosperity or high self-image. Think about the specific piece and materials used and how you felt wearing it. Consider your core values and commitments and how you display them. It might be time to stop saving them for special occasions and wear them proudly for all to see.

See also Crystals (page 62).

- What kind of jewelry did you see?
- Why was the jewelry noticeable in the dream?
- Was it yours, or did you gift it?
- What values do you hold close in your waking life?

Keys

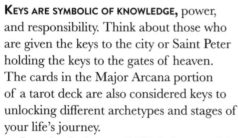

KEYS ARE SYMBOLIC OF KNOWLEDGE, power, and responsibility. Think about those who are given the keys to the city or Saint Peter holding the keys to the gates of heaven. The cards in the Major Arcana portion of a tarot deck are also considered keys to unlocking different archetypes and stages of your life's journey.

In order for keys to fulfill their potential, though, they must have something to open. What was your dream key connected to, and were you able to actually use it? Understanding what you were trying to open, and how much effort it took, can help you solve some of the problems and mysteries of your waking life. Finding the key is the hardest part—you're almost there!

See also Doors (page 71).

What did the key lock or unlock?

Who held the key?

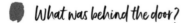
What was behind the door?

What's a problem you are working through in your waking life?

Knots

KNOTS HAVE BEEN A PART OF SPIRITUAL CEREMONIES across cultures and religions, and they indicate strong commitment. This includes weddings ("tying the knot," get it?). In an ancient Celtic tradition known as "handfasting," a couple binds their hands with a braided rope and exchanges their vows. During the Saptapadi ritual in Vedic Hindu wedding ceremonies, the couple's garments are tied together as they take seven laps around a sacred fire. The tied garments are a symbol of unifying two souls. Knots have deep theological significance in Jewish worship, specifically on the tallit, a prayer shawl. The 613 knots tied to the shawl's four corners remind wearers of the 613 commandments in the Torah. And ancient Egyptians believed that knots could bind or untie magic and signified eternal life.

Knots also serve the practical purpose of physical connection. A loose or untangled knot could mean life or death for a sailor or rock climber, and ancient Andean cultures used *quipu*, or collections of knotted strings, to collect numeric and statistical information.

How did the knot show up in your dream? Chances are, if you are in the process of untangling a knot in a dream, you are working out a problem in waking life. The gnarlier the knot, the more frustrating the situation. Think about what you are hoping to straighten out and what patience it may require.

What was tied up?

Did you untangle the knot?

What is going on in your waking life that needs to be untangled?

Are you making a long-term commitment in life?

Labyrinth

A LABYRINTH IS LIKE A MAZE, except it offers only one path to the center. That sentence alone evokes a myriad of metaphors for your dream. The most obvious one is that you are traveling a path toward enlightenment, to your soul. Many labyrinths are represented in a circular shape, such as a spiral, or some variation of a mandala. Jung, in his years of dreamwork, found his patients dreamed of mandalas and circular paths when they were seeking wholeness.

If you have dreamed of a labyrinth or mandala, your conscious self may be looking for a relationship with your subconscious world, opening up endless streams of creativity and connectedness. Pay special attention in forthcoming dreams for further symbols of circles, spirals, and paths, which are clues that you are headed in the right direction. They may not be obvious—this is where dream journaling could prove valuable.

See also Snail (page 129).

Did you reach the center or find your way out?

What obstacles did you face?

Was anyone with you?

What inner path are you on?

Light Bulb

THE INCANDESCENT LIGHT BULB made its way into people's homes and offices in the 1800s and has become a symbol of innovation and technological advancement. Light bulbs transitioned people from the days (and nights) of candlelight into a world of constant brightness. Think of all the things that can happen in the evenings, thanks to modern light. For better or worse, we no longer depend on the rising and setting of the sun to dictate our slumber.

If you turn on a light in your dream or see a bright light bulb, look at what you are working on, creatively and professionally, in your waking life. It's like that ah-ha moment when the light bulb flashes above a cartoon character's head. In your waking life, what needs illumination or clarity? Perhaps the bulb was shining a light on a clue.

But what if the bulb wouldn't turn on or burned out after giving a strong light? Consider your emotional stamina and capacity right now and try not to let your inner light dim. It might be time to replace your (metaphorical) light bulbs with something more energy efficient.

- How bright was the light?
- Did you have difficulty turning it on?
- Did you have an "enlightening" moment?
- What needs illumination or clarity in your waking life?

Lion

A COMMON SYMBOL FOR STRENGTH, courage, and nobility, the lion is one of the most recognizable animals across all cultures. It shows up in myths and folklore and has been immortalized for centuries in figures, such as the protective Sphinx in Egypt or, in modern culture, the characters in Disney's *The Lion King*. (Fun fact: *Simba* isn't just the name of the protagonist; in Swahili it means "lion" and "strength.")

In astrology, the Zodiac sign Leo is represented by a lion and ruled by the sun. Can you see the resemblance between a sun's rays and a lion's mane? Leos typically have a healthy sense of self-worth and are natural-born leaders.

Your instinctual and wild nature may be speaking to you through your dreams when the lion appears. It could be time to step into your power, harness your strength, and lead the pride!

- How did the lion appear?
- Was the lion fierce? Lazy? Was it hunting or at rest?
- What areas of your waking life need physical or emotional strength?
- Are you feeling pride over an accomplishment?

Lotus

LOTUS FLOWERS ARE BEAUTIFUL, sculptural aquatic plants that have the unique capabilities of maintaining a healthy temperature, thriving in low light, and removing toxins from water. More interestingly, lotus flower seeds can remain dormant for over a thousand years before blooming again. They are the national flower of Egypt, India, and Vietnam.

Because of their purification process and daily "rebirth," they are spiritual symbols in multiple religions, including Hinduism and Buddhism, and symbolize hope and perseverance. Lotus flowers can get dirty, quite literally, and emerge each day clean and unscathed. Zen Buddhist teacher Thich Nhat Hanh is known for saying "No mud, no lotus" to communicate that without difficulties, our life— the lotus—cannot flourish.

When a lotus flower shows up in your dream, it's a reminder to look at your whole self. The lotus's roots run deep, processing impurities yet projecting beauty. Think about how you process your own "dirt" and if it's time to make changes.

- Where did the lotus appear?
- What color was it?
- What are some areas in your waking life that need detoxification?
- How do you outwardly project your stress?

Luggage

- What was the condition of the luggage?

- Did you lose the luggage?

- What was inside it?

- What stresses and emotions are filling your brain in your waking life?

In waking life, luggage or a suitcase typically means upcoming travel. Depending on how you feel about traveling, this could be a dream come true or fill you with dread. Are you about to embark on a trip in your waking life? If so, then dreaming of a suitcase could be an extension of this event.

If no immediate trips are planned, however, consider the luggage or suitcase to be a symbol of something else: you. As with many vessels, like a cup or a house, something that can be filled is often a metaphor for you or someone in your life. Consider your emotions (or emotional baggage) and how you feel right now. Perhaps a situation in your waking life is difficult to carry and you need to unpack it, consolidate it, or lighten the load.

Mailbox

RECEIVING LETTERS IN THE MAIL can be such a thrill! When was the last time you sent a personal piece of snail mail? Or opened a mailbox to an unexpected surprise? When letters show up in your dreams, consider the vessel they are stored in: the mailbox. Vessels often symbolize portions of the body that can be filled, like the brain (which stores knowledge). If the mailbox was stuffed to the brim, your mind is probably busy and overly full with thoughts, tasks, and to-do items. If it's empty, you may be experiencing some emptiness of the heart.

What did the letter you received say, and how does that relate to areas in your waking life? Who was it from? Consider who you've been thinking about recently—and who you want to be thinking about you.

Finally, what was the state of the mailbox? If it was dusty and full of cobwebs from lack of use, it's time to break out a pretty piece of paper and connect with an old friend or relative!

● Where was the mailbox?

● Was the mailbox full or empty?

● What kind of mail was inside?

● What are you struggling to communicate with someone?

Makeup

FROM THE EARLIEST TIMES, people have added cosmetic layers to their faces for protection, camouflage, and intimidation. As people evolved, cosmetics became part of a beautification process and a symbol of status. Often far from natural, makeup accentuates or hides features, suggests arousal (flushed cheeks and red lips), and can be a bold personal statement. A painted face could very well mean glamour and confidence. But look deeper: Underneath those layers of added protection is your own beautiful face. Think about your insecurities in your waking life and about what you are covering up. What is this mask protecting?

As with many dream symbols, remember to think abstractly. The meaning behind dreaming of makeup could be in words alone: "make up." Is there something or someone in your waking life you need to make amends with?

○ What kind of makeup were you wearing?

● How did the final result make you feel?

● What are you trying to conceal in your waking life?

● What is something that needs to be gussied up?

Medicine

MEDICINE EXISTS IN A VARIETY OF FORMS, from natural herbs to prescribed drugs. It can be a touchy subject filled with controversy, but at its core, medicine exists to heal.

Use this dream of medicine as a symbol and an ah-ha moment! If you dreamed of missing a daily pill or the dream was associated with drugs you currently take, then it may be a straightforward anxiety dream, whether about your own health or your lack of control over it. But if the medicine showed up unexpectedly, take a look at your real physical and mental health needs right now and what you can do to heal any existing pain.

Quick fixes can only last so long, so you may need to make longer-lasting improvements in your waking life. Is now the time to take that creative writing class you've been thinking about or try practicing yoga? The medicine you need to feel whole again may look different than a typical pill. You know what they say—laughter is the best medicine. Why not write yourself a prescription for something that will bring you joy?

- What kind of medicine did you take?

- What were its effects?

- Did you have health problems in the dream?

- What is something causing you physical, emotional, or spiritual pain in your waking life?

Mirror

IN FAIRY TALES AND MAGIC, mirrors provide a gateway to peer into other worlds. And across many spiritual beliefs, they represent truth and light. In our own day-to-day existence, looking in a mirror can tell us a hard truth about the way we see ourselves. The mirror doesn't say a word (well, unless you are an evil queen) but instead offers an image to help us self-assess.

When a mirror shows up in your dream, try to remember your surroundings and who (or what) was reflected back at you. Was the reflection peering back a surprise? Maybe you were younger, older, or, in your eyes, prettier or uglier. The word "reflection" alone can help you gain insight on what your dream message is and what truths you need to hear!

Pay attention to the quality of the mirror. Was it shattered (a superstition indicating bad luck, or perhaps a symbol of your emotional state), or was it fogged up and hard to see yourself? If your reflection wasn't clear, think about your inner self and how your insecurities might be projected outwardly.

Where was the mirror?

Who or what was reflected in the mirror?

How did the reflection make you feel?

What in your waking life needs a fair, unbiased look?

Money

THE "MONEY CAN'T BUY HAPPINESS" IDIOM is a tough one to swallow. At its surface, you'd think that of course money can buy happiness, especially when you have financial stresses or a sudden influx of cash. Dreaming of money, though, can help bring to light the values money can't directly purchase. Look at your dream cash not as something to be used for an exchange of goods but as an abstract symbol of your emotional, physical, and spiritual wealth. Hitting the jackpot represents luck, abundance, or increased self-worth; finding your wallet unexpectedly empty indicates the opposite.

Where are you rich, and what areas could use some extra spending? Your "financial" health in these areas can manifest happiness in waking life, and knowing where you place value can possibly help you understand some of your waking life's financial goals.

- Did you find or lose money?
- How much was there?
- What did you do with the money?
- What are your needs like in your waking life?

Moth

MOTHS ARE THE NOCTURNAL COUSIN OF THE BUTTERFLY, and while similar in body structure and metamorphosis, they differ vastly in their cultural and daily significance.

Some moth species are considered pests, destroying crops and clothing, while others are used for their silk production during the cocoon stage. In many cultures, the moth is seen as a bad omen, a harbinger of death. It is said that if a moth flies into a room when someone is sick, that person will die—or, more positively, that the moth is bringing messages from someone who has recently passed away.

When a moth shows up, it might be symbolic of a transformation or journey. Moths are nocturnal and drawn to light, even at the expense of their own life. What is going on in your waking life that is catching your attention or that you are feeling drawn to? Is it something you need to turn away from to protect yourself, or is it something you need to run toward?

⚫ How did the moth appear in your dream?

⚫ Have you recently lost someone close to you?

⚫ What are you feeling drawn to in your waking life?

⚫ Are you going through any physical or emotional transformations?

Mountains

WITH THEIR PEAKS POINTING TOWARD THE HEAVENS, mountains have long been connected to the divine. In Greek mythology, the twelve Olympian gods lived on Mount Olympus. Moses received the Ten Commandments from God atop Mount Sinai. In many religions, mountains, such as Mount Kailash in Tibet, are dedicated sacred spaces housing temples and hosting pilgrims.

In their physical sense, mountains are immovable masses of great size and strength. They cast shadows and inspire humans to conquer new heights by climbing their steep slopes.

Dreaming of a mountain can be a numinous experience (page 15). Waking up from a mountain dream might leave you feeling a sense of awe. Think about your time on the dream mountain and what you were attempting to do. So much of our personal growth is about overcoming obstacles and learning, step by step. Did you summit the peak? Take a deep breath and look around, but don't feel too puffed up! Reaching the top is quite an achievement, but it doesn't put you above others—just closer to your highest, connected self.

See also Avalanche (page 35); Climbing (page 57).

● What were you doing on the mountain?

● Did you climb to the top?

● What challenges are present in your life?

● What inner journey are you currently on?

Music

THE EXTERNAL WORLD can definitely affect your dream state. For example, you've probably heard an alarm go off in your dream, only to realize the clock by your bed is beeping, too. Music can also do this, but what about dreams where music happens all on its own?

Whether you are tone deaf or a virtuoso, music is a source of inspiration, joy, and the divine. It sets the mood and helps tell a story—that goes for your dreams, too. Pythagoras, the Greek mathematician and philosopher, believed that music frequency was the sound of celestial bodies and that it connected our math, science, shapes, and sounds harmoniously. Consider the tone of what you heard and how it made you feel. Was it a romantic ballad or a jaunty melody? Or perhaps you heard something out of tune that left you confused or anxious. And if you're lucky enough to catch some lyrics, write them down! They may hold the key for something you are working out . . . or maybe you've just dreamed up a new song.

See also Audible Dreams (page 17).

What kind of music was it?

Where did it come from?

Had you heard it before?

What project needs to end on a high note?

Nudity

FINDING YOURSELF NAKED in front of a group of people is a common anxiety dream (or nightmare!). It's no surprise, seeing as nudity has an incredible number of connotations across cultures—the body, and how we see it, is both personal and political.

In Christianity, realizing your nakedness, like Adam and Eve did, was a result of the original sin of eating the forbidden fruit in the Garden of Eden. In Renaissance art, nudity symbolized the natural state, purity, lust, or poverty. Today, nudity evokes a variety of responses based on different cultural norms.

Once you get past the embarrassment (or thrill) of the nudity dream, take a look at what you are exposing too much of in your waking life and how it makes you feel. You may be suffering from a vulnerability hangover. Also pay attention to what does need to be stripped down to its minimal and natural state. This doesn't necessarily mean your naked body! Did you say too much at a party, or are you about to give an important presentation? Sometimes pubic (not a typo!) appearances can directly correlate with an anxiety-inducing event that's about to happen. Stand tall and proud and be comfortable in the skin you are in!

See also Sex (page 126).

Where were you?

Did you choose to be without clothes?

How did you feel?

What areas of your waking life feel too exposed?

Parades

TICKER TAPE PARADES, Mardi Gras, Pride, St. Paddy's Day. All reasons worth celebrating, right? Whether it's a neighborhood affair or a city-wide festival, parades are spectacles, often involving marching bands, floats, and grand marshals. What was your dream parade like? Is there something in your waking life worth celebrating, worthy of a miles-long procession?

Think about your role in the dream parade. Were you on the sidelines, wanting to join, or leading the band? And how did you feel about your role? This dream might be reminding you of your waking-life commitments and how active a role you play in the parts worthy of showing off.

- Were you a participant or a spectator?

- Did the parade have a theme?

- What was the weather like?

- What is something in your waking life worth showing off?

Parents

DREAMING OF PARENTS can vary from one person to the next, especially when you consider the dreamer's existing relationship with their family. Did your family appear exactly like themselves, or were they represented symbolically? Freud believed that parents can show up in our dreams as royalty and authority figures.

What traits did your parents have in the dream, and do they mirror the ones your parents have in waking life? Compare your dream interactions to interactions you have with those you care for. Are you acting as a guardian? Perhaps protectiveness is a quality that you may have admired in (or desired from) one of your parents? If not, how can you use your dream messages to enhance the qualities you feel you are lacking?

If your parents have passed away, what messages were they imparting in the dream? Was it a coping mechanism for their absence, or do you think it was a visitation from beyond?

Lastly, remember that dream symbols are often metaphorical and that dreaming of your parents might be a reminder to take care of yourself. What self-care routines and rules do you have in place? If none come to mind, what could you begin doing?

See also People (page 20);
Visitation Dreams (page 16).

● Which parent was it?

● How did they appear?

● What was your role in the dream?

● Who or what are you nurturing, protecting, and guiding?

Performing

THEY SAY THAT ALL THE WORLD'S A STAGE, but performing on one is a common anxiety dream. It usually goes one of a few ways: You nailed it and got a standing ovation. You forgot your lines. Something horribly embarrassing happened. Or nobody showed up to watch. Dreaming of being in the spotlight typically indicates the need for preparation. These dreams might show up the night before a big presentation or after an upsetting incident you didn't handle well. How you feel on stage may also reflect how you are feeling in your waking life, whether vulnerable and fearful or confident and proud. Like all anxiety dreams, use this one as a way to mentally prepare for the worst so that you shine like a star when the curtain rises.

- Why were you in the spotlight?
- How smoothly did it go?
- How did you feel in front of everyone?
- What "roles" do you find yourself playing in your life?

Phones

HOLD THE PHONE! The modern telephone connected voices in ways that changed communication forever. As it evolved into a mobile device, we came to use it less and less for actual phone calls and instead developed a genuinely addictive need for constant access to, well, everything.

Look at how a phone showed up in your dream and how clear the call was. Were you actually speaking to someone, or were you communicating through your thumbs? Connection to other humans is vital to our existence. Consider who you might be missing or who you want to spend quality time with. Who might need to hear your beautiful voice right now? Whose voice do you need to hear? If the call was dropped or hard to hear because of poor reception, it may be an indication that you feel disconnected from something in your own life—a core emotion, relationship, or event of importance or trauma.

If your dream phone was a modern smart device and scrolling through or using it caused negative emotions (stress, sadness, anger), perhaps it's quite simply time to unplug for a few minutes and make more tangible connections with yourself or loved ones.

- Who was calling whom?
- What kind of phone was it?
- How were you using the phone?
- Who is someone you need to communicate clearly with in your waking life?

Plants

ANYONE WHO HAS A COLLECTION OF HOUSEPLANTS or tends a garden knows that it takes a lot of patience and care to keep them alive and thriving. A symbol of nature, fertility, growth, and transformation, plants start from a simple seed and can develop into massive trees or beautiful flowers. They serve medicinal purposes as well as provide food, shelter, and even clothing. Dreaming of plants is a nudge to check in with your own personal growth and the patience it requires.

When you dream of plants, what is noticeable? New blooms? Hidden growth? Clumped roots or dry soil? Think about each part of the plant and compare it to your current life, and even your body. These dreams can be fertilizer for even more growth. What needs watering and sun, or what part of you can serve as a beautiful gift to brighten someone's day?

See also Corn (page 59); Lotus (page 100); Roses (page 121).

- What kind of plant did you see?
- How healthy was it?
- What was special about this plant?
- What areas of your waking life are currently experiencing growth?

Pregnancy/Birth

- Who was pregnant in the dream?

- What stage of pregnancy was it?

- How was the process? Painful, easy, comfortable?

- What projects or ideas are you gestating?

DEPENDING ON HOW YOU FEEL ABOUT PREGNANCY OR CHILDBIRTH, this dream could potentially give you a lot of anxiety. Yes, the dream could literally be about pregnancy, whether yours or someone else's. But it doesn't have to be. The physical act of being pregnant is one of creation. Think of how that symbolically relates to you. Perhaps you are in the early stages of a new project or life change. Ideas are growing, and you are starting to become protective, nurturing it within yourself until it is ready to be born and shown to the world. Pregnancy, both literally and figuratively, can be a fragile and emotional time period. There might be something—or someone—in your life that needs protecting.

If you've flipped to this page because you (or your partner) are, in fact, pregnant, you are in for a wild dream ride! Because of the physical, hormonal, and emotional changes coursing through your body, you may find your dreams to be heightened experiences. This is a perfect time to start dream journaling, if you haven't already.

See also Babies (page 37); Eggs (page 72); Spilling Something (page 132).

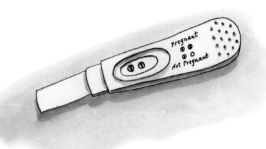

Rabbits

QUICK! BE VIGILANT. COORDINATED. KEEN. These are all traits of rabbits that you may need in your waking life, especially if a rabbit showed up in your dreams.

Rabbits have long been known for their breeding capabilities and, because of them, are often associated with sex. Due to their reproductive abundance, they also indicate prosperity; a rabbit's foot is a symbol of good luck, after all. And in the Chinese zodiac, the rabbit is a generous and likable creature. On the flip side, they are also seen as witty tricksters in folklore and literature or, like the White Rabbit in *Alice in Wonderland*, they might lure you into a new world of self-discovery.

Think about what you are fortunate to have and what, if anything, you are creating. How can you bring your desires to fruition?

- How many rabbits did you see?
- Were you a rabbit?
- Was the rabbit wild or domestic?
- What is abundant in your waking life right now?

Rainbows

AFTER A STORM COMES A RAINBOW. After a rough patch, hope. Because of their diversity in color and the fact that they are a refraction of light, rainbows have become a symbolic image of peace and good fortune. Communities across the world—including LGBTQIA+ members and Buddhists—use a rainbow flag as an identifier. Rainbows also serve as a celestial bridge in various religions and mythology, connecting heaven and earth. The Buddha was said to use a seven-colored staircase to descend back to earth.

The emergence of a rainbow is a mesmerizing thing. Notice when your dream rainbow showed up and what in your waking life needs more light, color, and hope.

See also Bridges (page 47); Colors (page 24).

- When and where did the rainbow appear?
- How did you feel when you saw it?
- Was anyone with you?
- What is something you are hopeful for?

Ram

AS THE MASCOT FOR THE ZODIAC SIGN ARIES, rams are animals bursting with energy and potential, known for their hardheadedness and determination. Their horns have been linked with sexual virility and fertility. In ancient Egypt, Khnum, a ram-headed man, was the god of fertility. Rams are also a sacred animal of the Greek god Hermes, who helped transition souls from the earth to the afterlife.

As with many animal dreams, think about whether the ram was communicating with you or if it was simply a symbol of something that needs attention in your waking life. What areas are causing you to butt heads with someone? Do you need to be hardheaded about it and force your way through, or is this a chance to sacrifice your pride, step back, and take a softer approach?

- Were you the ram? Or its shepherd?
- Did you notice anything specific about its appearance?
- What was its disposition?
- What is something you are stubborn about right now?

Roller Coaster

ORIGINATING FROM RUSSIAN ICE SLIDES in the eighteenth century, roller coasters have become an amusement park staple for adventurous thrill seekers. Constructed of wood and steel, new coasters are built each year and compete to be the fastest and steepest.

Roller coasters are often metaphors for life's ups, downs, twists, and turns. "I'm going through a roller coaster of emotions right now!" may be a familiar phrase to you. Think about what is going on in your waking life and how that relates to the roller coaster in your dreams. It might be time to relinquish control, let go of your fear, and enjoy the ride.

- How did you feel on the roller coaster? Safe, scared, excited?

- Who were you riding with, if anyone?

- Are you generally a risk-taker, or are you more reluctant?

- What adrenaline jolts have you experienced lately?

Roses

THE ROSE IS THE FLOWER OF APHRODITE and often associated with love. Like the lotus, it grows out of the mud and achieves earthly perfection, featuring layered petals that are luxuriously soft and fragrant.

Roses have been used in matters of the heart for centuries in love potions, spells, and fortune-telling. Many of us are familiar with games like "They love me, they love me not," where plucking petals determines whether a crush is interested in us.

They're also an important symbol in Christianity, often aligned with the Virgin Mary and used in miracles and messages from God. The rosary, used during prayer in Catholicism, is a string of beads or knots whose name translates to "garland of roses."

Color is significant when we peel back the layers of the rose's symbolism. Using floriography, we can identify messages within each color. Let's take a look at roses:

CRIMSON: Mourning, death

PALE PINK: Grace, joy

PEACH: Modesty

PINK: Happiness

RED: Love, passion

WHITE: Innocence, purity

YELLOW: Friendship, jealousy

How did the rose show up in your dream? Knowing that it's a symbol of love and devotion, is there a person or passion in your life in need of extra attention? Look closely at the health of the flower: A vibrant rose indicates current or forthcoming love, while a wilting rose reveals the opposite.

- What color was the rose?
- Did someone give it to you?
- Was it a cultivated rose or growing wild?
- What areas in your waking life could use extra beauty?

Running Late

THIS CLASSIC ANXIETY DREAM is up there with missing school (page 124) and being chased (page 41). In these types of dreams, obstacles are often put in your path to prevent you from succeeding. (You forget your luggage at home and have to go back, causing you to miss your flight, for example.)

If this type of dream shows up with no obvious connection (like an upcoming deadline, meeting, or event), look a bit deeper: What are you afraid of missing out on? Do you perhaps have a milestone birthday coming up and haven't hit some of your life goals? Does the thought of missing a party make you spiral into despair? Use this dream to ask yourself what would happen if you did miss out or if you didn't achieve what you set out to. Is there another opportunity to connect or try again?

See also Anxiety Dreams (page 18).

- Where were you going?
- What obstacles prevented you from getting there?
- Did you finally arrive?
- What timely projects or deadlines do you have going on in your waking life?

Salt

THERE'S A LOT TO UNPACK IN A TINY GRAIN OF SALT! At its simplest, salt is a mineral that enhances food's flavor. But there is so much more to it than that. Salt is essential to human life and can preserve foods for long periods of time. In ancient Rome, salt was used as currency, and it continues to be a part of religious ceremonies, purification rituals, and superstitions. Because salt exists in water yet evaporates and cumulates on land, it is seen as both a water and an earth element.

Think about your own connection with the mineral. Is there too much salt in your diet? Do you rely on it for sore-muscle soaks? Because it can be a symbol of either prosperity or bad luck, connecting it to your daily life is key. Salt in dreams can serve as a reminder to spice up your life if you're feeling a bit bland or, as the old idiom says, as a reminder to not take everything so literally, but rather with "a grain of salt." Preserve what's important to you, too, by writing down your thoughts and memories or sharing stories with friends and family members.

- Did you taste the salt?
- Where did you find the salt?
- Was the salt plentiful or scarce?
- What is something in your waking life that needs to be preserved right now?

School

WHETHER YOU ARE A CURRENT STUDENT or haven't seen the inside of a classroom for many years, chances are you've had a dream about school—and those dreams are rarely pleasant. Anxiety-inducing scenarios might include missing class, realizing you haven't turned in any assignments the entire year, being unable to find your classroom, or having a fling with the teacher.

Were you afraid of looking stupid in front of your peers or an authority figure? Was the hallway blocked and you didn't know how to reach your destination? Was learning a new subject excruciatingly difficult? Reflect on your current insecurities.

But there's a good part about school, too, and that's learning and the pursuit of knowledge. Think about what you need to learn about yourself. Or maybe the meaning is more external, and it's just time to pick up a new hobby or skill set that engages and challenges you.

If your dream focused on the building itself, consider the symbolism of houses (page 89) and see how it might be connected to your self.

- What were you learning? Were you prepared?
- Who was the teacher?
- Was the school a familiar one?
- What big project are you currently working on in your waking life?

Secret Rooms

FINDING A NEW ROOM IN YOUR HOUSE can be a common recurring dream, and usually a very exciting one to have! At its core, it's a dream of self-discovery and hidden potential. Consider in what part of the house you found the room. A room in the attic relates to your brain, where new ideas are waiting to be discovered. But a hidden crawl space deep underground could represent buried emotions or memories from your subconscious. So what does your secret room represent?

Think about what you are starting to learn about yourself or what is being revealed. Did you already know about this room in your dream and were keeping it a secret, or was it a surprise? Discovering this space might be a wake-up call for you, indicating that you need to do some inner exploration. Or, if you were the one doing the hiding, it might be time for you to open up and show off your talents.

- Where and how did you find the room?
- What was inside?
- Who else knows about it?
- What area of yourself are you starting to discover?

Sex

BEFORE WE DIVE IN, here's a reminder about other
people in your dreams: They don't always represent
the person they appear to be. Sometimes they
personify an idea, and very often they represent
you or an aspect of you, such as your personality.

Let's also note that having sex dreams is
completely normal, even if you were doing it with
someone that surprises you—an ex, a coworker,
a celebrity—or acting as a voyeur. In waking life,
sex is a healthy part of your mental and physical
wellness. It is a method of reproduction, a deep
connection between two people, and can be a lot
of fun.

Sex can also be connected with trauma and hurt, and if your dreams revolve around past experiences that cause nightmares or stress, consider seeking professional help to assist in healing.

We can't mention sex dreams without mentioning Freud. A large part of his dream analysis was centered on wish fulfillment and sexual repressions. By his theory, most of our dreams were sexual in nature but camouflaged by layers of symbols. By now, that should come as no surprise to you, dear reader. He did once (allegedly) say, "sometimes a cigar is just a cigar." Jung, on the other hand, took sex in dreams to be a unifying process of two opposites. In that sense, it can be a close connection with another person or an integration within yourself.

Regardless of who you slept with, think about the qualities and personality of that person. Are these areas that could use improvement in your own life? Remember, you might actually be sleeping with your subconscious!

- Who was your partner (or were you watching)?

- Were you satisfied?

- What personality traits do you wish you were more comfortable possessing?

- Where in your waking life might you be craving a deeper connection?

Smells/Scents

SCENT IS HARD TO DESCRIBE, but it can evoke instant memories and emotions in a way that other senses cannot. It serves as an intuitive and metaphorical tool—think of how it feels when you "smell something fishy." In your dream, did you smell something specific, or was it a scent memory? How does that scent relate to your waking life? In that regard, experiencing a scent in a dream is a wonderful way to explore a deeply embedded memory.

Not many people report being able to actually smell during dreams. Researchers say that dream scents are created by the brain and not from external factors. However, using aromatherapy can alter dreams depending on whether the scent introduced is sweet or foul. With this in mind, creating dream pillows to put next to your bed at night is a fun way to enhance your dreams (page 12).

● What did you smell?

● Did it smell good or bad?

● What memories are triggered by this smell?

● What are your senses trying to tell you?

Snail

THESE SMALL CREATURES HAVE A SURPRISING AMOUNT OF SYMBOLISM ATTACHED TO THEM. With their spiral-shaped shell, snails represent cycles and beginnings, particularly those related to seasons and lunar cycles. The emergence of the snail from its shell can also be symbolic of birth. Jung uses snails to symbolize the self, with the conscious as the hard outer shell and the unconscious as the soft body inside.

At the basic level, when we think of snails, we tend to think of their unhurried pace. When they show up in dreams, consider whether you need to slow down on a project or with a person in your waking life. Since we live in such a fast-paced society, take dreaming of such a slow-moving animal as a sign that you're in need of some stillness—even more so if you find yourself frustrated at the snail's leisurely speed.

- Were you the snail?
- Did you see the snail's trail?
- What is your current housing situation like?
- What needs to slow down in your waking life?

Snake

SNAKES ARE RICH IN MEANING. They are seen as both good and evil, male and female, life and death. The ouroboros, a common symbol of a snake devouring its own tail, sometimes in the figure eight, represents the birth and death cycle and its infinite loop.

In myths across cultures, snakes have keen intelligence and partner with evil, sometimes serving as guardians of the underworld. In the biblical story of creation, a serpent tempted Adam and Eve to eat the forbidden fruit. We often fear snakes, especially venomous ones; if this emotion shows up in your dream, you may very well be encountering a fearful situation or stress-inducing obstacle in your life.

Serpents slither forward and shed their skin multiple times a year, and because of this they are associated with change and transformation. They also represent intelligence and healing, and they appear on the caduceus, the staff of Hermes and a universal symbol of medicine. Kundalini—a dormant, powerful, divine feminine energy in tantra yoga—is represented by a coiled serpent.

Looking at how the snake showed up in your dream, and your response to it, can help you decide what message it was trying to convey.

- Where did you see the snake?
- Could you communicate with the snake?
- Did it bite you?
- What areas of your waking life are in transformation right now?

Solving a Mystery or Puzzle

WHETHER IT'S AN ELABORATE MURDER MYSTERY set in an old mansion on a hillside or simply you watching yourself put together a jigsaw puzzle with missing pieces, dreaming of problem-solving means your brain is hard at work. It's not going to stop just because you went to sleep! What projects are you working on in your waking life that might need a new approach? Consider finding a partner in crime to help you or flipping the puzzle upside down for a new perspective. Use this dream as the missing clue to finding new ways of solving your waking-life puzzles.

- What needed solving?
- Who helped you?
- What was the solution?

- What are some problems you are actively working on in your waking life?

Spilling Something

IN THE BUFFET OF LIFE WE CAN EASILY PUT TOO MUCH ON OUR PLATE, causing the gravy to spill off the sides, dripping onto the floor. This may be a cheesy metaphor, but we're talking about dreams and symbols, and that's how the sleeping brain works!

Usually when you spill something, it represents a loss of control or overflowing emotions. Whether you're clumsy or just carrying too much, something's going to hit the floor and be hard to recover. In your dream, look at what you were carrying and how it spilled. If it was fluid in nature, this is often a symbol of your emotions and subconscious. The vessel it was in can represent your body and brain.

Think about how you responded when you spilled something in your dream—how did you feel? Embarrassed, or relieved of a burden? Perhaps the spill was just what you needed to open up. Consider this dream theme a wake-up call to carry only what you can hold comfortably. There will be time to go back for more when your hands are free.

- What did you spill?
- What kind of vessel were you carrying?
- What do you have too much of right now?
- What are you struggling to hold in?

Stairs

IF WE USE THE THEORY THAT A HOUSE IS A SYMBOL OF OUR BODY AND SOUL, a set of stairs can represent so much: rising to the top, having multiple levels to our psyche, or overcoming an obstacle (like climbing a fourth-floor walk-up with a heavy bag of groceries!).

Stairs are also a common spiritual symbol. Across religions, ladders are used as symbols to connect heaven and earth. Angels and the Buddha alike used ladders, and in the Bible, Jacob had a dream about a ladder guiding him to God.

How did the stairs show up in your dream? Noticing their condition and whether you were going up or down can be very important, especially if we consider stairs as a tool of enlightenment. Walking confidently upstairs is an indication of progress, but walking up never-ending stairs is evidence that your journey seems Sisyphean. Going down or standing still? You may be experiencing self-doubt and fear of failure. Noticing how you feel during such a dream can be the key to your next step in waking life.

See also Climbing (page 57); House (page 89); Rainbows (page 118).

- Did you ascend or descend?
- Did you reach your destination?
- How much of your energy did it take?
- What intellectual or spiritual goals are you pursuing in your waking life?

Storms

AN APPROACHING STORM is a literal and symbolic device for a major change on the horizon—a lifestyle shift, or maybe something more emotional. Once the storm arrives, be prepared to get soaked! A lot may be coming your way all at once, and how you felt during your dream storm can prepare you for inevitable change.

Storms serve as metaphors and allegories throughout literature and art. A hurricane is used as a symbol to show the senselessness in nature and its disregard for human need, as in *Their Eyes Were Watching God* by Zora Neale Hurston. In Kate Chopin's "The Storm," a brief and raging storm represents a quick and passionate affair between two lovers, and in Edvard Munch's painting *The Storm*, we're left wondering if the main figure is in anguish over a physical storm or one brewing inside her own brain.

When the storm clears, look around. Did you act with grace under pressure, or are you picking up the pieces from an emotional outburst?

Different types of storms may give further insight as to what your dream could mean. Let's look at a few in more detail:

Floods

AFTER A LONG BOUT OF RAIN and storms can come the destructive flood. In Christianity, the flood from the book of Genesis washed away sin and was meant to be a reboot. In your dream, what storm passed, and what murky pool of emotions remains? Think about what it will take to clear away the water and restore what was submerged.

Hurricanes

HURRICANES ARE SLOW-MOVING, destructive forces of nature that, with a spiral shape and centered "eye," have an otherworldly feel. Because there are often multiple hurricanes happening simultaneously and lasting for weeks, they are identified by people's names—consider that in your dream, the storm may very well represent you or a person in your life. The English word "hurricane" stems from the names of powerful deities: the Mayan god of storms, Huracán, and the Taíno god of evil, Huricán. With its connotation of hard-hitting turbulence, a hurricane in a dream can be an indicator of worry, frenzied emotions, or being tossed about by the winds of change.

Rain

RAINY DAYS CAN BE DREARY, but symbolically we can see rain as washing away the grime, hurt, and negativity and allowing new thoughts and ideas to grow. The darker the sky and the harder the rain, the brighter you'll feel once it clears and the sun shines through. Perhaps at the end you'll find a rainbow, representing hope and good luck.

See also Rainbows (page 118).

Snow

A BLANKET OF FRESH SNOW IS a serene and peaceful image indeed, and it represents purity, calm, and quiet. But the cold and wet nature of snow as it hits your exposed skin can be harsh and brutal. Are you experiencing cold and icy emotions, either internally or from someone else? And do you have something warm to help you thaw out from the frigid climate?

See also Avalanche (page 35).

Tornadoes

THESE FUNNEL CLOUDS HAPPEN FAST, destroying anything in their path with very little time to prepare. When Dorothy encountered one in *The Wonderful Wizard of Oz*, it literally swept her off her feet, and she was transported to a new world. There she learned that she already possessed the strength she wished for. What whirlwind are you going through, and what deep inner strength can you bring forth?

- What kind of storm was it?
- Was anyone or anything harmed by the storm?
- How did you feel during the storm?
- What big changes are happening in your waking life?

Superpowers

HOW MANY TIMES HAVE YOU WISHED YOU COULD FREEZE TIME, teleport, or fly? Through lucid dreaming (page 18), these superpowers can become available to you with time and practice. Once you are able to master controlling your dreams, the world is your oyster!

But what if the powers in your dream are out of your control? When we dream of being able to do things we cannot do in waking life, it could be an imaginative expression of qualities we wish we had. Perhaps you dream of freezing time because you have too much on your to-do list and are struggling to do it all. Or maybe you have the power of invisibility because you are feeling unnoticed and want to do something to garner attention. Look at how the superpower could benefit your waking life and make adjustments so that you become your best, super self!

● What superpower did you have?

● How did you use it?

● Who knew about your powers?

● What areas in your waking life could benefit from a bit more oomph?

Swimming

WHEN YOU SWIM IN YOUR DREAMS, try to recall a few key details, like the water quality and how hard you had to exert yourself. Water (page 148) is often associated with our emotional self and our subconscious. So what is your dream begging you to notice when you are swimming through it?

If the water was crystal clear and in a luxurious pool, then you may feel at ease with your hidden thoughts. Enjoy your swim and ask someone to bring you another daiquiri! The harder we struggle against the current, though, and the deeper and murkier the water is, the more we are at odds with our emotions. If you treaded water in a tumultuous ocean, it might be time to start a meditation practice or otherwise get in touch with your inner feelings. Dream journaling is a great place to start.

- What kind of water were you in?
- What confidence and skill level did you have?
- Did you encounter any difficulties?
- How is your emotional well-being in your waking life?

Tattoos

TATTOOS, now a common form of self-expression, have had different significance throughout history. In ancient Egyptian culture, only women were tattooed, adorned with images of goddesses in hopes of easing and protecting mothers during childbirth. In Samoan communities, the application of *tatau* is considered a rite of passage into adulthood. On the other side of the world, Inuit women have elaborate facial tattoos to highlight their accomplishments and spiritual beliefs. Tattoos also have a darker side. Throughout history, they've been used for branding, such as to identify prisoners at several concentration camps, including Auschwitz, during World War II.

Regardless of intention, tattoos are (for the most part) a permanent addition to your body. Getting one is a commitment and visible evidence of individuality. When dreaming about new ink, think about whether you already have tattoos and what permanent statement you wish you could make right now.

- Who was getting the tattoo?

- What did the tattoo look like?

- What part of the body was the tattoo on?

- What public statement are you needing to make in your waking life?

Teeth

- What was the condition of the teeth?

- Were they your teeth or someone else's?

- What are your current stresses in your waking life?

- Are you biting your tongue or holding back thoughts you really want to share?

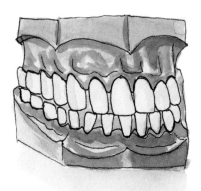

IN MANY SURVEYS OF RECURRING DREAMS, "crumbling teeth" is at the top of the list. And if you've had one of these dreams yourself, you may have spent the next few days running your tongue over your teeth to make sure they were still there.

Teeth are instant status symbols of good health and wealth and are also indicators of your mood. (Are you gritting your teeth? Smiling wide? Laughing so hard your gums are showing?) Throughout history, teeth dreams have been associated with distress, poor physical health, castration, and even an omen of a family member's impending death, according to the Jewish Talmud. With so many people across the globe experiencing this dream, we can safely say it's not a death prophecy. But do take a look at the stressors in your waking life—where you are feeling powerlessness—and practice relaxation techniques throughout the day. Your teeth will thank you for it!

Tightrope

WALKING A TIGHTROPE IS A DELICATE ACT OF BALANCE, training, and confidence, many times performed without a safety net. If you dream of walking across one, bravo! It is not for the faint of heart. Think about how you felt as you walked it and if you succeeded or failed.

If you fell, this does not mean you are a failure in waking life—far from it. Dreams can help show us what we are bothered by in our waking life, even if we don't consciously know it. Modern humans balance *a lot.* Jobs, families, social life, civic engagements . . . any one of these can wipe us out. If you have a lot on your shoulders at the moment, this dream will remind you to think about what areas are out of balance and what fine line you are walking to achieve your goals.

Who was walking the tightrope?

What was being carried?

Did the person walking the tightrope make it across?

What in your waking life are you juggling right now?

Time

BECAUSE OUR BRAIN WAVES SLOW DOWN in early dream stages of sleep (page 8), some doctors theorize that our dreams are processed at a different speed, as well. During waking hours, we have external stimulation to gauge time. In sleep all of that disappears, and our complex brains, unhindered by pesky reality, get to party.

But what about time as a dream theme? We can't master time in waking life, yet we try to control it, which often leads to much anxiety. What's most important is to breathe and do what we can with the time we have; to try to do too much in too little time can backfire and lead to burnout.

Time is precious. Did you find yourself going backward to revisit memories or correct wrongs in your dream? What are you trying to escape in your current life that makes you want to visit the past or future?

Dreaming of time is a great way to reexamine how you use yours. Is there never enough, or is it moving too slowly?

- How did time appear? Did you time travel, stop time, or simply see a clock?

- When did your dream take place?

- Do you have regrets about something that happened in the past?

- How do you spend your waking hours, and does this satisfy you?

Towel

WE MAY THINK OF A TOWEL as a large piece of fabric to help dry us off or clean up messes, but towels have been a symbol of respect and hospitality for ages.

In Christianity, a towel is symbolic of leading by example. Before sitting down with his disciples during the feast of Passover, Jesus removed his outer clothing and wrapped himself in a towel. He then washed the disciples' feet, drying them off with the towel he wore. In Japan, offering a hot, wet towel to restaurant diners and travelers is a strong part of hospitality culture. And to help rescue a boxer who is suffering in the ring, the boxer's team will throw in a towel to stop the fight. Douglas Adams writes in *The Hitchhiker's Guide to the Galaxy* that a towel "is about the most massively useful thing an interstellar hitchhiker can have" because of its practicality in all situations.

Think about the purpose of your dream towel. If it helped clean up a mess, think about what problems—or emotions, because we're talking about dreams—you are trying to solve, fix, or conceal in your waking life. If there wasn't a logical reason for the towel, think about how you could help someone else.

- What was the condition of the towel?

- Did you use the towel on yourself or someone else?

- What is something you feel negatively about? How can you clean it up?

- Is there something in your life you want to cover or conceal?

Transportation

PLANES, TRAINS, AUTOMOBILES, BOATS, and other forms of transportation can take us where we need to go—unless we get a flat tire, the map is wrong, or there are unknown detours. Dreaming of transportation vehicles helps you understand what your life's path is and what you need to move forward with. Pay attention to the details! What was the condition of the vehicle, how accurate were your directions, and who, if anyone, was traveling with you?

Many vehicles rely on the all-important wheel for propelling forward or steering. A mechanism of movement, wheels also represent cycles and the spinning of time: life, death, and rebirth. Who in your dream was in charge of steering?

Hopefully your dream was smooth sailing, but if you encountered obstacles, remember to think of them symbolically. They could be what prevents you from getting where you want to be in your waking life.

● What method of transportation was it?

● Where were you going?

● Did it arrive successfully?

● What is moving forward with or without your control right now?

143

Trapped

IF YOU DREAMED OF BEING TRAPPED, how did you handle it? Did you freak out? Look calmly at the situation? Take command of others in the room? Watch as they figured out an escape?

A trapped dream situation is an opportunity for you to try not to panic. Easier said than done, I know! Look around and focus on what is trapping you. Are you being buried alive, or do you find yourself in a room with no escape? When you wake up, think deeply about situations in your life that make you feel claustrophobic, anxious, stuck, or discouraged. It might be a job, relationship, or commitment, or the dream could just represent an overwhelming feeling of anxiety or frustration.

See also Jail/Imprisonment (page 93).

Where were you trapped?

Were you with other people?

Did you escape? If so, how?

What are some areas in your waking life that leave you feeling too confined?

Umbrella

YOU MIGHT HAVE BEEN TOLD that if you open an umbrella indoors, bad luck will rain down on you. This is a modern superstition. Historically, in Buddhism, an umbrella or parasol is a good luck symbol and offers protection from harsh elements and energies. Think about what (shade?) is being thrown your way in your waking life and what you can do to protect yourself from it. Alternatively, consider if the umbrella is your own protective mechanism against a flood of emotions or harsh elements. If the umbrella had holes in it, your emotions might be aching to get out. In that case, it may be time to close the umbrella and allow yourself to feel.

See also Rain (page 135).

- Was the umbrella open or closed?
- What condition was the umbrella in?
- What was the weather like?
- What are you needing an extra level of protection from?

Vacation

A TRAVEL DREAM can either be indulging or stressful, but regardless of the obstacles thrown at you or the number of piña coladas you drank, these dreams might be sending you an obvious message: You need a break! What is causing you a lot of stress in your waking life? A job? A relationship? Parenting? A mini-break could be beneficial.

Vacations and travel are restorative and eye-opening. Taking a monthlong trip to the shore might not be feasible, but odds are you can find some time each day for yourself: a quiet walk, a special meal you don't normally eat, or even that beach read you've been saving for your vacation. Your brain and body will thank you!

Where did you go?

Who was with you?

What was a high point in the vacation?

What are some routines you can break away from briefly?

Wasp

ARE YOU FEELING A BIT STUNG BY SOMEONE?
Or waspish yourself? Wasps, predator insects
that pack a powerful sting, can evoke annoyance
and fear. As a species, they use an intricate
communication system to protect their queen,
build nests, and forage for food. Wasps are
builders, fierce protectors, and quite threatening.

Their physical and personality traits lend
themselves well to describing people in many
situations. In modern society, WASP is an
acronym for a White Anglo-Saxon Protestant,
describing a social class of Americans who have
largely held the economic, political, and social
power—aka "the establishment."

But they have another side, too: Wasps can
show up to remind us of balance, opposites, and
striving for excellence. They are the antithesis to
the friendly bumblebee. What was the wasp doing
in your dream, and how did you respond to it?
The presence of this insect might be suggesting
that you be gentle with your words and wary of
those who could sting.

- Where was the wasp?
- Did you get stung?
- Did you hurt or kill the wasp?
- Who or what in your waking life is a possible annoyance or threat?

Water

As one of the basic elements, water is essential to life. Our lives begin in a watery world, deep inside the womb, and our bodies are made up of over 70 percent water. Because of this, water is a common symbol of life, growth, birth and rebirth, and creation. Water takes on the shape of whichever vessel it is in. In tarot, water is associated with the Cups suit and represents emotions.

In dream symbolism, Jung believes that water is the most common symbol of our subconscious. Through water dreams, our hidden thoughts and emotions are symbolized in a natural state. Look carefully at these dreams. They signal a time of undergoing emotional change, learning new ideas, and truly looking at your intuitive self. Regardless of how the water manifested, think about how clear, how deep, and how still or turbulent the water is. Then look to your emotional health and what might be going through some turmoil. Here are just a few ways that water might appear in your dreams.

Oceans

Oceans are vast and deep, full of mystery and opportunity for discovery. When you dream of oceans, consider it an ah-ha moment to "dive deeper" into your intuition and let yourself be submerged in your subconscious thoughts. New ideas will surely emerge.

Did you meet any sea creatures? Animals that live in the ocean are reflections of our hidden (or submerged, perhaps) thoughts and emotions. They are special dream visitors delivering messages from the depths of your soul. Did a multiarmed octopus remind you of all the helping hands you require, or did the great white shark remind you to constantly move forward? There are more than 200,000 known species living in the ocean, so do some extra research on the animal that visited you, and take note if it shows up in other ways in your waking life.

Now let's talk about waves: If water represents your emotions and subconscious thoughts, waves are the surge that can move them forward. Think of how we experience some emotions: waves of gratitude, or fear, washing over you. The more turbulent the dream waves, the harder you are pushing against yourself, whether you know it or not. These powerful forces of nature are inevitable, and it's up to you whether you get trapped beneath them or ride them out with fun and excitement.

Rivers

A CONSTANTLY MOVING BODY OF WATER, rivers are natural barriers, as well as pathways. Once on a river, you either go with the flow or fight the current, swimming upstream. What obstacles, if any, stood between you and your destination? Or, alternatively, was the river dry and barren? It might have been easy to cross, but at what (emotional and intuitive) cost?

See also Bathing (page 39); Spilling Something (page 132); Storms (page 134); Swimming (page 137).

How did the water appear?

What was the quality of the water?

Was the water contained in a vessel?

How easy is it for you to "go with the flow"?

Weddings

FOR BETTER OR WORSE, in sickness and in health, weddings symbolize a lifelong commitment between two people. In earlier centuries, weddings were less about love and more about political and financial gain and ensuring a family lineage. Some of the traditions and symbolism from early weddings still exist: exchanging rings, throwing a bouquet of flowers, and having a best man or maid of honor.

Wedding dreams show up in a variety of ways, including: being a guest at a wedding, marrying a stranger or someone you don't love, marrying someone you love, or planning a wedding.

Ultimately, use a wedding dream as an opportunity to think about commitment. The more active a participant you were in the wedding, the more willing you are to move forward with life's next big transition. As for the people in the dreams, remember that they can represent an idea or a personality trait you admire (or loathe). What project or relationship are you working on in your waking life that could cause this dream, and what level of control do you have? Think about the details (jewelry, colors, flowers) from the wedding and see if they offer any insight, as well.

Who was getting married?

How did you feel about this union?

What elements from the wedding stood out?

What are some commitments you are making in your waking life?

Werewolf

WE'VE PROBABLY ALL FELT LIKE WE'VE HAD AN INNER BEAST IN US waiting to come out and attack the residents of a small English village under the light of a full moon. Right? Whether you've felt this inner beast or not, dreaming of a werewolf could suggest that you have a dark, wild, or uncontrollable side. If you are thinking "What!? Not moi!"—think again!

Consider how werewolves are often portrayed as the bad guy in fairy tales, trying to hide their true form, but only for so long—transformation is inevitable when the full moon comes around. If these werewolf dreams become nightmares, address them head-on. The more you can acknowledge that there are parts of your personality you aren't happy with, the easier it is to confront them and make healthy (shape) shifts.

- Were you the werewolf?
- Did the werewolf attack?
- What was the transformation process like?
- What character traits are you hiding from the rest of the world?

Windows

A HOUSE WITH NO WINDOWS WOULD BE A DARK, musty, closed-off space. Windows bring us fresh air and natural light and let us look outside at the world beyond (unless your view is the brick wall of the building next to you). Dream windows provide a similar metaphor: They allow us perspective, enlightenment, and opportunity. When we consider the house as a symbol of our body and soul, the windows can help open up new ideas (or close them off) from our subconscious. Think back to the details of the window, where it was located, and what was on the other side of it. Are there opportunities in your waking life for new ideas?

See also House (page 89).

● Was the window open or closed?

● Were you looking in or out?

● What was on the other side?

● What opportunities are being opened to you?

Zombie

WANDERING AIMLESSLY. Dead eyes. Emotionally unavailable. Craving human flesh. Do any of these characteristics apply to you or someone you know (minus the last one)? Zombies, in dreams and pop culture, can be terrifying. The thought of being attacked violently and then turning into a being without a spirit or soul is a nightmare (and many a Hollywood movie) in the making.

The term "zombie" originated when West Africans were enslaved and brought to Haiti by the French. The West Africans believed that when a person died from unnatural causes, a bokor or caplata (male or female witch doctor, respectively) could revive the person during the limbo of time between life and the afterlife, but the creature would be left with no mind of its own.

When zombies show up, they are symbolic of our worst fears. Look at what is causing you stress and worry and think about how you can face it with energy and intention.

See also Being Chased (page 41).

Where did you see the zombie?

Were you attacked by the zombie?

What stresses are you unable to control in your waking life?

In what parts of your waking life do you feel like you're just going through the motions?

Notes

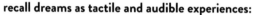

Chapter 1: The Philosophy of Dreams

rapid eye movement (REM) sleep, common to all dreamers: B. Herlin, S. Leu-Semenescu, C. Chaumereuil, and I. Arnulf, "Evidence That Non-Dreamers Do Dream: A REM Sleep Behaviour Disorder Model," *Journal of Sleep Research* 24 (2015): 602–609, https://doi.org/10.1111/jsr.12323.

recall dreams as tactile and audible experiences: H. Bértolo, T. Mestre, A. Barrio, and B. Antona, "Rapid Eye Movements (REMs) and Visual Dream Recall in Both Congenitally Blind and Sighted Subjects," *Proceedings of SPIE* 10453 (2017): 104532C-1, https://doi.org/10.1117/12.2276048.

seen as living representations of spiritual forces: "The Iroquois False Face Society," Native American Netroots, November 28, 2010, http://nativeamericannetroots.net/diary/787.

Even children's dreams are valid and listened to: D. Barrett and P. McNamara, *Encyclopedia of Sleep and Dreams: The Evolution, Function, Nature, and Mysteries of Slumber* (Westport, CT: Greenwood, 2012).

"It is not good to see the earth scorched or black . . .": Steven M. Oberhelman, "The Diagnostic Dream in Ancient Medical Theory and Practice," *Bulletin of the History of Medicine* 61, no. 1 (1987): 47–60, https://www.jstor.org/stable/44433662.

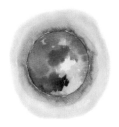

seeing them at play in our waking life: R. Robertson, *Beginner's Guide to Jungian Psychology* (Newburyport, MA: Nicolas-Hays, 1992), 106.

Chapter 2: The Science of Dreams

dreams are visual, emotional, or motor-based: M. Walker, *Why We Sleep: Unlocking the Power of Sleep and Dreams* (United Kingdom: Scribner, 2017).

neurochemical process occurring only during sleep: A. Robb, *Why We Dream: The Transformative Power of Our Nightly Journey* (Boston: HMH Books, 2018), 31.

that dreams can be a source of creative problem-solving: Kaitlyn Luna, "The Science of Dreaming," *Speaking of Psychology*, American Psychological Association, December 2018, streaming audio, 50:45, https://www.apa.org/research/action/speaking-of-psychology/science-of-dreaming.

Chapter 4: The Variety of Dreams

enhanced their connection with the departed: Joshua Black, Teresa DeCicco, Corrine Seeley, Anthony Murkar, Jade Black, and Patrick Fox, "Dreams of the Deceased: Can Themes Be Reliably Coded?" *International Journal of Dream Research* 9 (2016): 110–114.

dreamers recall other people speaking to them the most: Roar Fosse and Frank Larøi, "Quantifying Auditory Impressions in Dreams in Order to Assess the Relevance of Dreaming as a Model for Psychosis," *PloS One* 15 (March 2020): 3 e0230212, https://doi.org/10.1371/journal.pone.0230212.

people tend to report more anxiety dreams:
Colleen Walsh, "What Pandemic Dreams May
Come," *The Harvard Gazette,* May 14, 2020,
https://news.harvard.edu/gazette/story/2020/05
/harvard-researcher-says-dreams-indicative-of-virus
-fears/.

upcoming issues we may need to address:
Remy Melina, "Why Do We Have Nightmares?"
Live Science, July 28, 2010, https://www.livescience
.com/32730-why-do-we-have-nightmares.html.

Chapter 5: Symbols and Themes

Attacks: R. Robertson, *Beginner's Guide to Jungian
Psychology* (Newburyport, MA: Nicolas-Hays, 1992).

Corn: Marilou Awiakta, *Selu: Seeking the Corn Mother's
Wisdom* (Golden, CO: Fulcrum Publishing, 1994).

to protect the deceased in the afterlife: Joshua Mark,
"Egyptian Mortuary Rituals," Ancient History
Encyclopedia, March 11, 2017, https://www.ancient
.eu/article/1022/ancient-egyptian-mortuary-rituals/.

in Ayurvedic medicine: Vasant Lad, *The Complete Book
of Ayurvedic Home Remedies* (New York: Harmony Books,
1998), 276–283.

Feathers: Tristan Picotte, "The Significance of
Feathers in Native Cultures," *Partnership with Native
Americans* (blog), September 17, 2019, http://blog
.nativepartnership.org/the-significance-of-feathers
-in-native-cultures/.

Illness: M. Heid, "The Science Behind Fever Dreams,"
TIME, June 11, 2019, https://time.com/5603196
/fever-dreams-science/.

During the early days of the COVID-19 pandemic: "Why COVID Dreams Are Weirder Than Normal," *SciFri*, October 3, 2020, 17:03, https://www.science friday.com/segments/covid-dreams/.

Jail/Imprisonment: Sarah Vickery, "UWM Psychologist Finds Link Between PTSD and Prison," *UWM Report*, May 29, 2015, https://uwm.edu/news/uwm -psychologist-finds-link-between-ptsd-and-prison/.

Jewelry: M. Mancini, "Why Are Wedding Rings Worn on the Left Hand?" Mental Floss, January 4, 2017, https://www.mentalfloss.com/article/69315/why-are -wedding-rings-worn-left-hand.

a symbol of unifying two souls: Anusha Chellappa, "Saptapadi: All that you need to know about the seven steps of marriage," The Art of Living, n.d., https://www.artofliving.org/in-en/lifestyle/culture -and-heritage/know-about-seven-steps-of-marriage.

remind wearers of the 613 commandments in the Torah: "Tallit: The Jewish Prayer Shawl," Chabad.org, n.d., https://www.chabad.org/library/article_cdo/aid /530124/jewish/Tallit-The-Jewish-Prayer-Shawl.htm.

Nudity: P. Kolsoki, "Nudes in Sacred Art Contain 4 Types of Symbology," Aleteia, July 17, 2017, https://aleteia.org/2017/07/17/heres-why-the -sistine-chapel-has-so-much-nudity/.

School: Peter Gray, PhD, "They Dream of School, and None of the Dreams are Good," Psychology Today, June 29, 2016, https://www.psychologytoday. com/us/blog/freedom-learn/201606/they-dream -school-and-none-the-dreams-are-good.

Smells/Scents: Dany Mitzman, "Do People Experience Smell in Their Dreams?" BBC, May 28, 2014, https://www.bbc.com/news/magazine-27590756.

Tattoos: Cate Lineberry, "Tattoos: The Ancient and Mysterious History," *Smithsonian Magazine*, January 1, 2007, https://www.smithsonianmag.com /history/tattoos-144038580/.

Zombie: Zachary Crockett and Javier Zarracina, "How the Zombie Represents America's Deepest Fears," *Vox*, October 31, 2016, https://www.vox.com /policy-and-politics/2016/10/31/13440402/zombie -political-history.

Resources

A Dictionary of Symbols by J. E. Cirlot

The Interpretation of Dreams by Sigmund Freud

The Encyclopedia of Crystals by Judy Hall

Man and His Symbols by Carl G. Jung

The Wild Unknown Archetypes Deck and Guidebook by Kim Krans

Making Herbal Dream Pillows by Jim Long

The Illustrated Signs & Symbols Sourcebook by Adele Nozedar

Beginner's Guide to Jungian Psychology by Robin Robertson

A Field Guide to Lucid Dreaming: Mastering the Art of Oneironautics by Dylan Tuccillo, Jared Zeizel, and Thomas Peisel

Why We Sleep: Unlocking the Power of Sleep and Dreams by Matthew Walker

Acknowledgments

THE DREAMERS OF THE WORLD, both past and present, who have valued dreams personally, culturally, and scientifically have contributed far more to this book than I could ever acknowledge in one page. I truly hope that, through their wisdom, I helped shine a light on all the amazing capabilities our dreams can provide.

Without Crystal Moody's "Year of Creative Habits" workshop, this project may have never seen the light of day. A heartfelt thank-you to Crystal for her mentorship and for always inspiring me beyond my wildest dreams.

My writing group, The Split Nibs (Ingrid Bohnenkamp, Sarah Jenkins, and Susan Mann), keeps the creative momentum going. The night I expressed wanting to give up, they wouldn't let me. The following day, Anna Cooperberg serendipitously reached out, hoping to develop my dream project into a book.

Anna's grace and vision are seen throughout these pages. I am also so thankful for everyone at Workman Publishing who believed in this project and created

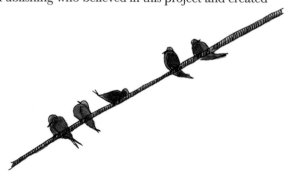

the best version possible: Orlando Adiao, Rebecca Carlisle, Diana Griffin, Moira Kerrigan, Dylan Julian, Kate Oksen, Barbara Peragine, and Susan Bolotin, and proofreaders and cold readers Zoe Maffitt, Martha Cipolla, Meredith Clark, and Shaina Crump.

As with most creative projects, there are countless people who served as cheerleaders, pre-readers, and collaborators. I thank you all for the support and for sharing your waking and nightly dreams with me. A few who have gone above and beyond include Emily Austin, Corey Kilburn, Janae Hardy, Kelly Knauer, John and Karen McQueary, Kristine Ruyle, the Springfield Regional Arts Council staff, and members of the Well Fed Head book club.

Thanks to my family, for allowing (and encouraging!) me to talk about my dreams nonstop: my twin sister Stephanie (and the whole Hornickel crew), the Chiltons and the Vermules, and, of course, my mom, Nancy, and my dad, Bob. Lastly, to Dan, Jasper, and Maggie: I love you!

About the Author

NICOLE CHILTON is an artist and writer who relies on the power of dreams to inspire creativity. She lives in Springfield, Missouri, with her husband and two children.

You can find her online at nicolechilton.com and on Instagram @nicole.chilton.art.